WITHDF

THIS NOBLE WOMAN

OTHER BOOKS IN THE
WOMEN OF ACTION SERIES

Bold Women of Medicine by Susan M. Latta

Code Name Pauline by Pearl Witherington Cornioly,
edited by Kathryn J. Atwood

Courageous Women of the Civil War by M. R. Cordell

Courageous Woman of the Vietnam War by Kathryn J. Atwood

Double Victory by Cheryl Mullenbach

The Many Faces of Josephine Baker by Peggy Caravantes

Marooned in the Arctic by Peggy Caravantes

Reporting Under Fire by Kerrie L. Hollihan

Seized by the Sun by James W. Ure

She Takes a Stand by Michael Elsohn Ross

Women Aviators by Karen Bush Gibson

Women Heroes of the American Revolution by Susan Casey

Women Heroes of World War I by Kathryn J. Atwood

Women Heroes of World War II by Kathryn J. Atwood

Women Heroes of World War II—the Pacific Theater
by Kathryn J. Atwood

Women in Blue by Cheryl Mullenbach

Women in Space by Karen Bush Gibson

Women of Colonial America by Brandon Marie Miller

Women of Steel and Stone by Anna M. Lewis

Women of the Frontier by Brandon Marie Miller

A World of Her Own by Michael Elsohn Ross

THIS NOBLE WOMAN

Myrtilla Miner and Her Fight to Establish
a School for African American Girls
in the Slaveholding South

MICHAEL M. GREENBURG

CHICAGO
REVIEW
PRESS

Published by Chicago Review Press Incorporated
814 North Franklin Street
Chicago, Illinois 60610
ISBN 978-0-912777-09-2

Library of Congress Cataloging-in-Publication Data
Names: Greenburg, Michael M., author.
Title: This noble woman : Myrtilla Miner and her fight to establish a school
    for African American girls in the slaveholding South / Michael M.
    Greenburg.
Description: Chicago, Illinois : Chicago Review Press Incorporated, [2018] |
    Includes bibliographical references and index.
Identifiers: LCCN 2017040095 (print) | LCCN 2017044969 (ebook) | ISBN
    9780912777108 (adobe pdf) | ISBN 9780912777122 (epub) | ISBN 9780912777115
    (kindle) | ISBN 9780912777092 (cloth)
Subjects: LCSH: Miner, Myrtilla, 1815–1864. | Women educators—United
    States—Biography. | African Americans—Education—History—19th century.
    | Antislavery movements—United States.
Classification: LCC LA2317.M524 (ebook) | LCC LA2317.M524 G74 2018 (print) |
    DDC 371.829/9607309034—dc23
LC record available at https://lccn.loc.gov/2017040095

Interior design: Sarah Olson

Printed in the United States of America
5 4 3 2 1

For my sister, Gail Richardson—a lifelong educator

CONTENTS

PROLOGUE

---•◆•---

TO PRESERVE A MEMORY

The Gilded Age of railroads and factories swept across America in the mid-1870s. Reconstruction, the process of admitting the Southern states back into the Union after the Civil War, had helped to rebuild a fractured nation, and slavery was but a sad and shameful memory, abolished with the flourish of Abraham Lincoln's pen and the blood of many. Myrtilla Miner had been dead since 1864. Her legacy, overshadowed by heroes such as Frederick Douglass, Harriet Tubman, and William Lloyd Garrison, seemed to fade as the years passed.

A writer and friend of Myrtilla's by the name of Ellen O'Connor—Nelly, as she was known to friends—was saddened by the waning memory of Myrtilla's work. Ellen knew that the fight to bring justice to African Americans before the Civil War had taken many forms and often extended far beyond the cause of abolition, a movement to end slavery. Myrtilla, the daughter of poor white farmers from Madison County, New York, had done her part to bring human rights and dignity to African Americans through the gift of education. She had traveled to Washington,

1

DC, a hotbed of slavery and racial tension, and bravely opened a school for African American girls. "Myrtilla Miner [was] one of the heroines of the irrepressible conflict," wrote US senator Henry Wilson in 1874, "not because she figured largely upon the theatre of popular discussion, or entered her public protest against the evils of slavery, but because in the humble walks of the lowly she quietly sought out and with patient and protracted effort educated the children of the proscribed and prostrate race." Senator Wilson viewed Myrtilla as someone who in her own quiet and humble way helped African American children—and the nation as a whole—through education.

Ellen O'Connor was determined to tell the world about her friend's work and decided to write a book about her. "I loved her very much," she wrote to Myrtilla's brother Isaac in 1886, "& felt that the story of her heroic labors here ought to be told."

The famous poet Walt Whitman was a longtime friend of Ellen's. He described her as "a superb woman, without shams, brags; just a woman." In the early 1850s she'd worked as a journalist for the antislavery newspaper *The Liberator*, as well as with the women's rights journal *The Una*. Later in life, when asked to defend herself as an "equal suffragist," one who supported equal rights for women including the right to vote, Ellen said that she was "one at birth" and that simple justice required no defense.

She had shared many interests with and known many of the same people as Myrtilla. Through the years Myrtilla had visited Ellen and her husband at their home in Philadelphia and then in Washington, DC, and the two women had developed a close bond. "The love & affection which you express for me I fully reciprocate, & then I have a feeling of resting upon you as I have upon no one else," wrote Ellen in an 1861 letter to Myrtilla. "I long sometimes for any body to think or act for me, but you are the only one who ever does."

Myrtilla spent the last years of her life in California, returning to Washington, DC, in 1863 only after being gravely injured in a horse and carriage accident. As she lay dying in the Washington home of a mutual friend, it was Ellen who passed hours of each day comforting her, tending to her correspondence, and listening to Myrtilla's stories. Inspired by Myrtilla's years of struggle to bring education to African Americans, Ellen became personally involved in carrying her friend's work forward for future generations. She dedicated herself to Myrtilla's cause and in the years following Myrtilla's death became a trustee of the Miner Fund, an organization formed to carry on the work of African American education. In this role, Ellen came to know many of Myrtilla's friends and former students and learned more and more about her friend's life. She was, perhaps, the perfect person to tell Myrtilla's story.

And so, in 1875, as economic progress spread across the nation leaving most African Americans behind, Ellen began to research the records and papers that detailed Myrtilla's life. She reached out to as many of her friends from different points of her life and career as she

Ellen "Nelly" O'Connor, close friend and biographer of Myrtilla Miner. *Feinberg-Whitman Collection, Prints & Photographs Division, Library of Congress, LC-DIG-ppmsca-07372*

could find. She interviewed family members, distant relatives, and business associates. She collected letters written by and to Myrtilla, and she studied newspapers, essays, and personal statements composed about Myrtilla and her work. The difficult task took years to complete.

Among the many notable people Ellen contacted in preparation for her biography of Myrtilla was Frederick Douglass. A runaway slave from Maryland, he had become a nationally famous speaker and writer and the leader of the American abolitionist movement. Knowing that Myrtilla had once sought him out for support of her school, and that his help writing her friend's biography would be valuable, Ellen wrote to Frederick on many occasions asking for his thoughts and memories of Myrtilla and her work. Finally, on May 4, 1883, he responded:

> You have often urged me to tell you the little . . . I remember of Miss Myrtilla Miner, the founder of what is now the Normal School for Colored Girls in the City of Washington. [A "normal" school is a school that trains teachers.] The task is, in every sense, an agreeable one.
>
> If we owe it to the generations that go before us, and to those which come after us, to make some record of the good deeds we have met with in our journey through life, and to perpetuate the memory and example of those who have in a signal manner made themselves serviceable to suffering humanity, we certainly should not forget the brave little woman who first invaded the city of Washington, to establish here a school for the education of a class long despised and neglected.
>
> As I look back to the moral surroundings of the time and place when that school was begun, and the state of public sentiment which then existed in the North as well

as in the South; when I remember how low the estimation in which colored people were then held, how little sympathy there was with any effort to dispel their ignorance, diminish their hardships, alleviate their suffering, or soften their misfortunes, I marvel all the more at the thought, the zeal, the faith, and the courage of Myrtilla Miner in daring to be the pioneer of such a movement for education here, the District of Columbia, the very citadel of slavery, the place most zealously watched and guarded by the slave power, and where humane tendencies were most speedily detected and sternly opposed.

Slowly, the fragments of information Ellen gathered began to take shape, and soon the story of Myrtilla Miner came to life.

A COUNTRY GIRL

At times the pain was more than she could bear. A frail and sickly child, Myrtilla Miner worked on her father's farm in North Brookfield, New York, harvesting the hops that were so important to her family's livelihood and the economy of the community where they lived. The cone-shaped crop, which was picked each autumn, provided the flavoring for beer and other beverages and required long periods of manual labor for its harvest.

Myrtilla's pain resulted not just from hard work under harsh conditions but also from grave health problems. She had been born with a spinal infection that required constant drainage and bandaging, and she suffered from tuberculosis, a lung infection that causes severe coughing and sometimes death. These conditions would ail her for much of her life. As a child her features remained animated despite her ill health, but her brown eyes often appeared sunken and her skin ghostly pale. She was thin and fragile for most of her childhood, and at times her family doubted that she would survive. An inner strength, however, lifted her and helped her to endure. Here, in the hills of Madison County, Myrtilla Miner did survive and learned to dream of a better life.

She was born on March 4, 1815, to Seth and Eleanor Miner and was, according to the family Bible, the fifth of twelve children. Her friends and family members called her Myrtle. Her parents were hardworking and devoutly religious settlers of a region described as "little more than an unbroken wilderness." They had migrated to New York from Connecticut and, like other New England pioneers, settled in the southeastern region of the county originally called the Nineteenth Township. Seth had chosen a parcel of land on the east side of a trail later known as Mill Hill Road for the site of his cottage.

By the time Myrtilla was born, the village of North Brookfield had been established and the community had begun to flourish. Seth helped found the First Day Baptist Church in Brookfield and also served as a lieutenant in the Madison County militia. In North Brookfield, wrote Ellen O'Connor, "the family was subjected to all the privations incident to the lot of early settlers. They grew up strong men and women, with little education from schools, but with habits of industry and economy, which were transmitted to their children, accompanied by principles of high moral integrity and deep religious reverence."

Myrtilla described her home in North Brookfield as a "curiously poetic part of the earth." The family cottage was situated on a rising bluff of Mill Hill "that we might take a copious view of the scenery and from that know whether it was best to laugh or cry, make poetry or prose." North Brookfield, she wrote, was "a land of hills and vales, greatly diversified and subject to extreme poverty and, consequently, very romantic."

The town was inhabited by at least one African American family—that of a prominent businessman named Laban Olby—but full racial integration was still years away. The enslavement of African Americans was, in fact, prevalent in both the North and South sections of the United States at the time. Olby was free and owned a popular local tavern and hotel. There is no evidence that he experienced the kind of violent racial discrimination that many black people suffered throughout the country. Myrtilla sadly pointed out, however, that North Brookfield was sometimes called "Nigger City" "on account of its peculiar locality and the queeritiveness of its inhabitants."

Myrtilla's father was a simple man who respected the traditional values of hard work and frugal living. He encouraged his children to learn the local trades or follow in the family business of farming. Girls, of course, were expected to become homemakers and to learn about taking care of families. Education beyond the mere basics was not practical with such a large family, and it was all but discouraged by Seth Miner. He was, according to Ellen O'Connor, "a man of uncommon natural ability, but, from his narrow training, regarded mental culture, beyond a certain limit, as superfluous and unnecessary." But Myrtilla was an intelligent child and, despite—or perhaps because of—her frail health, yearned for something more than what her hands could craft. She developed a free spirit and a passion to improve herself through education. "You wonder," wrote young Myrtilla of her home, "what intellectual fruit such a place could afford."

As a child, she was fascinated with the beauty of nature and made careful study of the physical world around her. "There is nothing upon which the eye of a Christian rests with more exquisite delight than natural scenery," she later wrote. Her family kept a small collection of books at home, and she read all that she could. She also borrowed books from friends and relatives, and though she often suffered with back pain, she worked long hours in the hops farms of Brookfield during harvest season to earn money for the purchase of her own books.

Myrtilla's formal education began at home. Her aunt, Ann Miner, founded a small school for some of the town's children and conducted classes at the Miner cottage. In time Ann gave up her small class, and Myrtilla enrolled in the district school located about half a mile from her house. The daily walk was difficult. The roads were little more than dirt trails, and the terrain was rocky, uneven, and very steep. The incline from her home was so abrupt that on several occasions her momentum caused her to fall to the ground and bump her head.

Once she completed the difficult portions of her daily journey, Myrtilla would enter the little town and make her way to the district school. The schoolhouse was located in a valley, and its rustic image appeared much like a 19th-century postcard. "Here I could see four dwellings, two churches, a black smith's shop, a carriage maker's shop and the old . . . antiquated school house," she remembered. "At the foot of the hill is the old red colored school-house ornamented with an attachment of sheds." The focus of the tranquil scene, however, was not, according to Myrtilla, the school building but the two nearby churches that lay not 25 yards apart from one another. "So long as the opposition church was in vogue the voice of the speaker in one could easily be heard in the other, sometimes the language distinctly."

———————•◦•———————

As Myrtilla began her education she immediately realized that girls were taught differently than boys of the same age—or not taught at all. In the early 1800s women were viewed as inferior to men and lacking in academic ability. Women had very few rights and were dominated by men at almost every turn. About half as many women as men could read. Women could not vote, in some cases could not own property, and were discouraged from expressing political or business views. Once married, women lost almost all legal rights to their husbands.

Education for girls was generally informal and not taken seriously by the male-dominated American society. Though Myrtilla was taught to read and write in the district school, female education in the early 19th century usually focused on domestic training and household chores such as taking care of children, preparing meals, and running a family. Even Thomas Jefferson, the third president of the United States had written, "A plan of female education has never been a subject of systematic contemplation with me." Plain and simple, he, and many like him, never thought about the issue.

In contrast to the norms of the day—and much to her father's disappointment—Myrtilla had little interest in domestic or household matters. She loved to read books and wanted to learn as much as she could beyond her own family and village. So indifferent to everyday items of fashion or girlish pursuits was Myrtilla that she even sewed together her multiple undergarments into one pullover sheath in order to save the extra time it took for her to dress each morning.

Though Myrtilla loved being at school she was often perplexed by the limited resources and opportunities available for girls. The inadequacy of female education in America frustrated her and kindled in her a sense of justice and a desire to make change. Why, she wondered, should girls not be given the same opportunities as boys to learn and to advance their education? During her school years, Myrtilla first acquired what she would later call "the principles of independent action"—an inner drive that would inspire her to action in the face of opposition.

As poor as education for white women was in the early 1800s, education for African Americans was far worse. In some regions of the country, even free black people—whose families had been enslaved and persecuted for generations—were discouraged from reading, and it was against the law for enslaved people to attend school. While white women began wondering about *equal* rights, black Americans suffered with virtually *no* rights. Though she did not realize it as a child, the anger that Myrtilla felt for gender bias would soon extend to racial bias, and the two together would come to define her life's work.

By age 15 or 16, Myrtilla understood that the best way for her to change the system was to join it. She began teaching other young children at the district school and was eager and enthusiastic about her work. Teaching was one of the only professions that women were encouraged to pursue beyond homemaking. From the start, Myrtilla was at home in a classroom. While some young women her age began to think of boys and ultimately marriage, Myrtilla's frail health and single-minded focus on books and study made dating and courtship unlikely. She enjoyed the company of boys, but her disinterest in housekeeping and child rearing seemed to make her an unlikely bridal candidate. Though she would fall in love several times in the coming years, it seemed that marriage was not in the cards for Myrtilla.

By 1835 she was teaching in nearby Oneida County near her brother David's home, but her thirst for learning did not stop just because she was a teacher. She knew instinctively that she would have to continue her education in order to be the best teacher that she could be. "This could only be done," she wrote, "by training the mind."

In the early 1800s a growing movement in favor of women's rights gave birth to a series of private girls' schools called seminaries. These institutions began to gain acceptance not only because of changing attitudes toward women but also due to a belief that a broad education would make women more skilled wives and mothers.

In the fall of 1839, when Myrtilla was 24 years old, she applied for admission to the Young Ladies Domestic Seminary located in Clinton, New York. There she hoped to further her education in a wide variety of subjects with the goal of passing on her learning to her future students.

The school tuition was $120 per year, and in what may have been a first-of-its-kind program, each student was expected to provide manual work in return for room and board in a type of work-study setting. Myrtilla had very little money to pay the other required fees and expenses. She begged the principal and founder of the school, Rev. Hiram H. Kellogg, to allow her to delay payment until after she resumed earning enough money as a teacher—and was ultimately accepted on that basis. "It was indeed, pathetic to see this young, frail girl, with her pale face and lustrous eyes, pleading for an entrance to the halls of learning," wrote Ellen O'Connor, "and perhaps it was the consciousness of this that influenced [the principal] to accept her conditions."

She and her father traveled to the seminary in Clinton on a cold November day in 1839. Such was Myrtilla's excitement at beginning her new adventure that she completely forgot to say good-bye to her father and thank him for transporting her and all of her things to the school. The head teacher, Mrs. Tompkins, greeted Myrtilla at the door and quickly shuffled her off to a warm room where a fire was burning in an open hearth. There Myrtilla sat alone listening intently as students in an adjoining room of the house recited poems and addresses for their teacher. Seth Miner no doubt stewed in the cold outside as he waited for a farewell from his daughter, but when Myrtilla

Female Seminaries

Female seminaries represented a growing trend in the early 19th century toward expanding women's rights and education. At a time when formal educational opportunities for women were scarce, seminaries, or female boarding schools, provided a broad range of academic subjects taught by well-trained instructors. The goal of these schools was to offer women a liberal education beyond the simple district schools, allowing them to be not only better wives and mothers but also useful members of society in general. Despite the broad message of gender equality espoused at these institutions, the student body was composed almost exclusively of white women. Educational opportunities for black women lagged far behind. Many female seminaries evolved into four-year colleges and provided women with training equal to or better than what was offered to men. Women were often trained at seminaries to be teachers for the many students attending the new public schools that were sprouting up throughout the United States. The seminary movement was fueled by an understanding that equality for women was a requirement of American society and that education was a central focus of that equality. How could women compete on an equal footing with men if they were not provided with equal educational opportunities? This was the question being asked by 19th-century women's rights advocates and educators such as Mary Lyon, Emma Willard, and Catharine Beecher. Each of them fought for the educational rights of women and helped to build the movement of female seminaries in America.

finally realized her blunder it was too late. The only way to the front door was through the occupied classroom, and she was not about to intrude on the students' meticulous narrations!

"I doubt not my father felt not a little chagrined when he found that after all his pains to transport me here he was left without any expression of thankfulness or parting salutation," she wrote. Then, in resignation, she added, "I had no remedy only to let my forgetfulness pass for a mistake and make the best I could of it."

When the class finally ended and Seth had long departed, the entire school of nearly 40 students, Myrtilla included, gathered in a large circle and was led in a 10-minute physical exercise period. Mrs. Tompkins, it turned out, was a distant relative of the Miner family, and later in the day she and Myrtilla sat down and talked like old acquaintances.

Myrtilla was given a room on the third floor attic of the building, and since this required her to climb many steps (elevators having not yet been invented), she was temporarily excused from the kitchen duties usually required of all students. Miss Fowler, the matron of the school in charge of student well-being, was aware of Myrtilla's health problems and assured her that as soon as possible she would be given a room on the lower floors.

In a very short time Myrtilla settled into a rigorous schedule. The students were woken every morning by a clanging bell at 5:00, and by 5:15 they were gathered in the schoolroom for worship and the singing of Christian hymns. Prayer and religious devotion entered nearly every part of the day. Meals began with prayer and song, and the students were encouraged to study Bible passages and repeat Sunday school verses. Each student was given kitchen or household chores, and each was expected to join in group physical exercises and personal study time in addition to classroom work. Myrtilla reported that her studies included arithmetic, chemistry, philosophy, composition, and astronomy—a class that she eloquently called "geography of the heavens." The typical school day ended at precisely 8:30 pm, and lights were expected to be out by 9:45. In a letter written to her family during the first few days at the seminary, Myrtilla cheerfully reported, "Health pretty good—friends a plenty." In a signal, however, of the obvious nerves that went along with her new experiences she signed the letter, "My mother's anxious child, Myrtle Miner."

One afternoon Myrtilla gazed out her bedroom window at the Young Ladies Domestic Seminary and marveled at the quaint and beautiful setting below. She was so impressed by the scene that she recorded her impressions in a school essay, describing the area as "rich and pleasing in the highest degree." The essay provided a wonderful glimpse into 19th-century life in Clinton, New York, through the window of Myrtilla's third-story bedroom:

> The street which leads to the village is lined on each side with neat cottages, with green blinds and pleasant yards. These are ornamented with shrubbery and children. The latter are busily engaged in the sports of a delightful summer evening. Upon the walk may be seen ladies devoted to pleasure walking and seminary girls without bonnets. A lady rides up street on horse-back, but quite too slow for me. Three ladies ride down in a carriage, driving a cunning little pony. An old gentleman and his young wife come out into their yard to look at the shrubbery. They appear as loving as kittens.

The tranquil calm of Clinton, however, hid an ugly reality in the United States. Throughout the South, African Americans were enslaved and forced to work against their will on the farms and in the homes of Southern plantation owners. Enslaved people were given no rights and were often abused. They were regarded as property to be bought and sold to the highest bidder and often separated from their family members when it suited the purposes of their masters. Across the country—even in the North—free black citizens were discriminated against and were, for the most part, prevented from working with or associating with white people. Racial inequality, whether through slavery or segregation, was part of American culture and had been since the birth of the nation.

Despite this widespread injustice, many white Americans refused to engage in discrimination and many others, often at much risk, welcomed their black neighbors into their towns, homes, and schools. Indeed, among the 40 or so students enrolled at the Young Ladies Domestic Seminary in 1839 were several African American girls. Reverend Kellogg was a devoted abolitionist,

Rev. Hiram H. Kellogg, founder of the Young Ladies Domestic Seminary in Clinton, New York. "They were received as others were," wrote Kellogg of the African American students whom he admitted to the seminary.
Special Collections and Archives, Knox College Library, Galesburg, Illinois

and though schools that allowed black students in the same classroom as white ones were rare at the time, Kellogg did not hesitate. "They were received as others were," he wrote in 1841. "I chose to regard and treat them as <u>pupils</u>, not as <u>colored pupils</u> . . . and allow me here to say, that my confidence was not misplaced." It was probably in Clinton that Myrtilla established her first relationships with African American women and learned the lessons of fairness and racial equality. She developed compassion for powerless people and an understanding of those who struggled with hardships.

While in Clinton, Myrtilla first learned of Gerrit Smith, a leading abolitionist, politician, and social activist. She came to admire Smith's work and, upon learning of his failing health, wrote him an anonymous letter complimenting his dedication and urging him to get well so that he could continue his battles for the underprivileged. It was an early sign of Myrtilla's social awakening.

Not long after Myrtilla's arrival at the seminary her health began to decline again. "I was quite sick for a few days after I arrived," she wrote to her younger sister Achsa. "My back was so sore I could scarcely move or stir." She was examined by a local doctor who concluded that she was suffering from inflammation and an infection along the spinal cord. She had no choice but to undergo an agonizing procedure described by Ellen O'Connor as "the heroic kind," in which setons, or drainage canals, were inserted into her back to remove accumulated pus. "I think . . . the remedy is worse than the disease," Myrtilla confessed to her sister.

Myrtilla was bedridden and unable to go to classes or eat with the other girls in the days and weeks following the procedure. Twice a day her kindhearted roommate changed the dressing on her spine and slowly nursed her back to health.

Gerrit Smith

Gerrit Smith was born on March 6, 1797, into a wealthy family in Utica, New York. Throughout his life, Smith amassed a fortune in real estate, becoming the wealthiest landowner in New York State at the time. He actively supported the temperance movement—a campaign against the consumption of alcoholic beverages—and was a staunch advocate for women's rights. By 1835 Smith became a fanatical abolitionist, and he used much of his fortune to support the movement. He lived frugally so that he could give money to the less fortunate. According to the National Abolition Hall of Fame, Smith gave away nearly $8 million in the course of his lifetime to antislavery causes—about $1 billion in today's money! His home in Peterboro, New York, became a well-known stop for those escaping slavery through the Underground Railroad. In 1840 Smith played a major role in the creation of the Liberty Party—a political party dedicated to the antislavery movement—and he was nominated for the presidency in 1848 and 1852. He was elected to the US House of Representatives in 1852 but, frustrated with the lack of change in Congress, resigned his seat in 1854. Smith fervently supported those who fought against slavery, but the strain sometimes proved more than he could take. In October 1859 he suffered a mental breakdown and was committed for several weeks to an insane asylum. He died in 1874.

Remarkably, Myrtilla managed to remain current on her studies during those difficult days, keeping pace with her classmates.
Friends brought books and assignments to her room, and she
continued her schoolwork despite the excruciating pain in her
back. Through the kindness of others and her own firm determination, Myrtilla was able to move beyond her frailty and continue her growth as both a student and a teacher.

As the summer of 1840 approached, Myrtilla's health was
much improved, and she considered leaving Clinton to resume
her teaching career. Unsure of what to do, she asked Reverend
Kellogg, whose opinion she greatly valued, what he thought of
the idea. Kellogg inquired how she was feeling and suggested
that if she had an opportunity to teach and was feeling up to it,
he would not object to her leaving. Her doctor advised her to
remain for the summer, however, fearing that travel and stress
would strain her too much. Though she was feeling better, the
setons in her back prevented any strenuous work or activity. She
decided to continue her studies at the seminary, but in September 1841 her mother, Eleanor, died, and Myrtilla was forced to
return home to take care of the family.

Though once again involved with household matters at the
Miner cottage, Myrtilla never stopped thinking about education
and the unfairness of the school system toward women. What
began as a feminist impulse would one day merge with a desire
to bring equality to the races. For now, however, she focused on
educational opportunity. Feelings of anger began to stir within
her, and soon she developed a political and activist mindset.

If change was to occur, she reasoned, *she* would be the instrument and *now* would be the time.

AWAKENING

Shortly before Christmas of 1841, Myrtilla wrote a bold letter to the governor of New York, William H. Seward. In the coming years Seward would become a US senator, a presidential candidate, and the secretary of state under President Abraham Lincoln, but in 1841 Governor Seward was the highest-ranking state official in New York and in charge of many important public matters.

"Will you, sir, with all the multitude of cares that press upon you . . . devote to the subject of <u>Female Education</u> a few thoughts?" wrote Myrtilla. "By a little observation, you will discover, that . . . [poor] females find it almost impossible, to obtain means of acquiring sufficient knowledge to render them competent . . . or capable of training their offspring as the necessities of our beloved country require." Myrtilla had studied Seward's annual message to the legislature from the previous year and had been disappointed to find no reference to education for girls. She respectfully accused the governor of being out of touch with women who felt the "anguish of an irrepressible thirst for [education], without means to quench it," and she angrily asked why there were plentiful colleges in the United States dedicated to educating men but few if any such institutions for women. She closed by asking Seward for his thoughts on the matter—and, in time, his influence and action.

To Myrtilla's surprise, Governor Seward quickly replied to her letter. In one short paragraph without detail or specifics he told her that while much work remained to be done on female education he was pleased with the state's progress on the issue thus far. That was it. He did not address Myrtilla's concern about college for women. He did not recognize the plight of poor women and their lack of educational opportunities. And he certainly did not acknowledge Myrtilla's passion on the issue. In short, Myrtilla viewed the governor's brief letter as an insult to her and the many women who suffered from inferior education, and she stewed with anger and frustration over what she saw as ignorance on the issue.

Myrtilla's correspondent William Seward. He served as governor of New York, US senator, and secretary of state under President Abraham Lincoln. *Prints & Photographs Division, Library of Congress, LC-USZ62-21907*

As she struggled with how best to respond to the governor, Myrtilla's thoughts returned to continuing her own education. Her family had begun to recover following Eleanor's death, and Myrtilla supposed it was time to move on with her life. To further her goal of teaching, she traveled west to Rochester, New York, where she enrolled at the Clover Street Seminary, a private girl's school established in the late 1830s as an alternative to the city's district schools. With money in short supply and personal debts rising, Myrtilla quickly switched from student to teacher, and by December 1842 she was instructing a class at the seminary of "40 young Ladies—the loveliest in the land." Now firmly settled in Rochester and inspired by what she called "the overpowering responsibility of a teacher," she once again wrote to Governor Seward.

"Perhaps you will recollect receiving a letter . . . from Myrtilla Miner," she began. "To that letter, you gave a short reply which was duly rec'd, & fully appreciated—but unfortunately for you not satisfactory to me." Then, in a bold and angry tone, she proceeded to scold the governor of New York for not fully appreciating the plight of women in the context of education.

"You seem to express more pleasure for what <u>has been</u>, & <u>is being</u> done, than <u>regret</u>, for what is not done," she wrote. "[And] you do not tell me <u>why</u> there are no institutions for females, corresponding with the many collegiate schools scattered over our country for gentlemen. Why is this? Will you tell me?" She wondered openly whether, in fact, the male-dominated society purposely *intended* that women not be educated, and she questioned why male teachers earned more money than female teachers. "Their education costs no more than mine—then why so vast a difference in remuneration?" And in a truly forward-thinking proposal, Myrtilla suggested to the governor that New York create a system of schools for women with reduced tuition costs to reflect the lower pay received by women in the work-place. "My heart aches for the <u>many</u> who are situated . . . with an unquenchable thirst for knowledge," she concluded. "They may be now weeping tears of sorrow, over the ignorance they have it not in their power to banish from their minds."

Despite the scathing tone of Myrtilla's letter, Governor Seward again very promptly and kindly replied. He complimented her "maturity of thought" and admitted that he could not offer a sat-isfactory reason why female education had been ignored by the state. "It may suffice however that no one more sincerely deplores that error than myself," he added. Seward declared his support for public colleges for women and stated that society could only move forward if women were "relieved from . . . inequalities . . . and promoted to higher power and influence." Even as Seward left office at the end of 1842 without any real change in female access to education in New York, he made it clear to Myrtilla that he was her friend and ally in the cause for women's rights. The two would, in fact, write letters to each other for years to come.

Through her assertive letters to Governor Seward, Myrtilla had become an advocate for women's education. She had identi-fied injustices that had been part of the American system for so long that most people didn't even recognize them as such, and she sought to change that system—not just for herself but for the betterment of those around her. "My sympathies are always attracted to that class whose disadvantages most require them," she wrote.

———•◦•———

As motivated as she was to help women, Myrtilla constantly bat-tled with her own poverty as well as a restless spirit that often left her unhappy and searching for something better. She sometimes

William Seward

William Henry Seward is best remembered as secretary of state under President Abraham Lincoln. Born in Florida in May 1801, Seward developed a strong antislavery attitude early in life. He studied law, moved north to New York, and soon became interested in politics. In 1830 he was elected to the New York State Senate and served as governor of the state from 1839 to 1842, where he first became acquainted with Myrtilla Miner. As a devoted abolitionist, Seward was elected to the US Senate, where he served from 1849 to 1861 and proudly fought against slavery. As the Civil War approached, he sought the Republican nomination for president but was beaten by Abraham Lincoln, who upon election appointed Seward as his secretary of state. He became one of Lincoln's most trusted advisors during the war and until the president's assassination in 1865. Remaining at his post after the war under President Andrew Johnson, Seward negotiated the purchase of Alaska from Russia in 1867. He died in Auburn, New York, in October 1872.

---

found it hard to focus on one issue for long periods and, as demonstrated by her letters to William Seward, was often touchy and impatient with the people she associated with. Her abrupt and occasionally difficult personality made it hard for her to hold a job even though she was capable and dedicated to her work. At times, conflict with others made reaching her goals seem unlikely.

Sometime in 1843 Myrtilla left the Clover Street Seminary and began teaching in the school system of Rochester. She became the highest-paid teacher at District School No. 6 but still made only enough money to survive, leaving most of her debts unpaid. Soon she was involved in a conflict with the directors of the school, and she grew unhappy with her job. To make matters worse, she agonized over a crumbling romantic relationship with a man. She complained bitterly to her brother about her loneliness and the isolation she felt in Rochester. "Now don't begin to talk any more about nobody loving you," he responded. Disenchanted with the city and saddened by her personal situation, Myrtilla decided that she wanted to leave Rochester. She wrote to friends and relatives asking about any open positions but quickly learned that New York teaching jobs were in short supply—and teaching jobs were about the *only* jobs open to women.

During that time, Myrtilla began thinking about continuing her teaching career in the South. Later in life she would claim that her opposition to American slavery and her desire to view it personally was behind the idea. The truth, however, was much more practical; she desperately wanted to leave Rochester and had been told that there were many more teaching opportunities in the Southern states. She began to research schools in the South and told her friends and family members about her thoughts. Their responses would again send Myrtilla in an unexpected direction.

Throughout 1844 she had been writing letters to her cousin Mary Atwater, who was then living in Providence, Rhode Island. Mary had been saddened by the death of a friend, and she begged Myrtilla to come to Providence. She was quick to add that teaching jobs were available in the city. "Just come on and I will almost ensure thee success," wrote Mary.

Mary's husband, Stephen Atwater, was a city civil engineer and friendly with the superintendent of the Providence school system. Stephen reported to Myrtilla that Providence officials were actively looking for qualified teachers from other cities and that the superintendent had shown great interest in hiring her. "He told me the last time I saw him and he stopped me on the sidewalk on purpose, that Miss Miner could have a place even now if she should come on," Stephen wrote. Knowing that Myrtilla had been exploring teaching opportunities in the South he added this prophetic warning: "Now banish forever your notion of going to the South—the treacherous South. She may allure you by the promise of a generous reward, but if she gets you within her unhallowed arms . . . she will abuse you. . . . Don't trust yourself to her for an hour. She is deceitfull [sic] above all things and desperately wicked."

Myrtilla decided to follow Stephen's advice and, for the time being, put away thoughts of traveling south. By the end of 1845 she began teaching at the Richmond Street Intermediate School in Providence and, more importantly, came to learn about the most modern teaching methods in the country.

Under Henry Barnard, the state superintendent of schools in Rhode Island, Myrtilla was introduced to new and innovative approaches to public education and funding. Known as the "scholar of the educational awakening," Barnard brought European techniques to the school systems of the state, established a series of town libraries, and went on to become the first US commissioner of education. The great educator Horace Mann called Barnard's Rhode Island school plan "one of the best systems of public instruction in the world."

While in Providence, Myrtilla also expanded her feminist views and, through the Atwater family, met with many people from New England who were active in the most debated topics

Horace Mann

If you attend a public school, chances are you have Horace Mann to thank for it. Known as the "Father of the Common School" because of his strong support of and leadership role in public education reform, Horace Mann began his career first as a lawyer and then as a lawmaker in his home state of Massachusetts. In 1837 he was elected as the secretary of the Massachusetts Board of Education and became the strongest voice in the movement to guarantee a free basic education—funded by tax dollars—to every child. Born into a poor family and spending most of his childhood in poverty, Mann found whatever learning he could in the local library and, for the most part, educated himself. At age 20 he was admitted to Brown University, where he began to understand the link between politics and education reform. Mann came to understand the vital need in a democratic society for a thriving educational system open to all, regardless of social class or religion. In 1838 he began publishing a periodical called *The Common School Journal* to instruct teachers in the most up-to-date methods, and he lectured about these methods and on the need for public education in general. In 1848 he was elected to the US Congress, where he continued to fight for the cause of education and the abolition of slavery.

of the day. Feminists and those who supported equal rights for women were often associated socially and politically with people who embraced other causes for change, and Myrtilla became friends with those people.

Public education was but one of many types of reform taking root in the United States in the 1840s, and Myrtilla developed a social awareness of these movements. Religion, nutritional improvements, workplace reform, women's rights, and, of course, slavery were the hot-button issues in the nation, and Myrtilla seemed to be naturally drawn to these causes and the people who guided them.

While teaching in Rochester, she had been introduced to the antislavery activist William R. Smith, and she tutored children—some African American—in his home during her vacation time. Rochester and its surrounding towns had become a focal point of abolitionist activity and served as a way station of the Underground Railroad—an alliance of sympathetic citizens dedicated to the protection and movement of people fleeing slavery. Myrtilla was exposed early on to the arguments against slavery and to those who zealously promoted those arguments.

Dedicated abolitionists such as Henry Ward Beecher and his sister Harriet Beecher Stowe had a profound effect on Myrtilla and helped to mold her political views. She read their literature and admired their acts of courage in opposing injustice. And in time she would come to understand the vital role that a simple teacher could play in the fight against slavery.

———•———

Myrtilla had developed a free and independent spirit that would serve her well in future years. Working in Providence at the age of 30 she couldn't help but look back at her life with some level of satisfaction. As a result of her frail health, Myrtilla's family had desperately worried about her ability to make it alone in

The Underground Railroad

The Underground Railroad was a secret network of people and routes dedicated to helping enslaved people escape to freedom. It was not a railroad in the physical sense, nor was it underground, but it was responsible for the movement of an estimated 100,000 African Americans to Canada or free Northern states from 1810 through 1850. The system used many terms associated with actual railroads; escape routes were referred to as "lines," safe houses or stops were called "stations," and kind people who assisted along the way or during escapes were called "conductors." The most famous "conductor" of the Underground Railroad was Harriet Tubman, who had escaped slavery herself yet bravely returned to the South on many occasions and guided hundreds of people to safety and freedom. Fugitive slaves typically traveled at night and moved from station to station, where they were given food and shelter by caring citizens. All of this, of course, required great organization and cost lots of money, and so the Underground Railroad was managed and funded by many generous philanthropists and antislavery activists dedicated to the cause of freedom.

the world, but she was proving that she could at least live on her own and take care of herself.

She had become a role model for her younger sister Achsa, who was now leaning toward a further education of her own. Encouraged by Myrtilla to continue her schooling, Achsa showed great promise, and the two hoped to one day work together as teachers. Their hardheaded father, however, did not share the girls' enthusiasm. "I tell you positively," he wrote to Achsa, "I shall never support you with her . . . to have the name of educating her sister. I have my hands full other ways & for myself I have doubts whether it is best for you ever to undertake a high school course." Seth Miner wondered whether his daughters would not be better served in the more traditional roles of farming and motherhood.

Despite a clear conviction in her work and a self-confidence that drove her forward, Myrtilla remained restless and unhappy even in Providence. Perhaps she recognized the injustice of vast improvements in public education for white children while black children remained enslaved in Southern states. Great advances had been made, but in some ways the country was as backward as it had ever been. For the most part, Northern schools remained segregated and education for African Americans was either flawed or nonexistent. And in many parts of the South it was all but illegal to teach black children. Myrtilla was bitterly frustrated that she had gained a broad education but could not share her knowledge with those most in need. Years later she recalled, "My attention was called to the subject of American Slavery and feeling no satisfaction in its contemplation I became exceedingly desirous to travel and teach in the South in order that I might see it as it would appear to me."

MISSISSIPPI

Myrtilla's work in the Providence school system brought her in contact with some of the great minds in the educational movement. New methods of teaching and of sustaining public schools were sweeping the nation, and a fresh, open-minded attitude of the importance of publicly funded education had taken root. Among the pioneers in this cause was William B. Fowle of Boston, Massachusetts. A loyal follower of Horace Mann, Fowle was said to have been the first to use blackboards in the classroom, written spelling lessons, and the monitor system, which allowed advanced students to instruct the less capable. Under Fowle, physical punishment of students by instructors, which was common in the early 19th century, came to an end.

As the publisher and editor of Horace Mann's *Common School Journal*, a magazine that promoted the important role of government in the education of children, Fowle's work was very familiar to Myrtilla. As she began searching beyond Providence for a more suitable teaching position she wrote to him to let him

William B. Fowle, a pioneer in education, informed Myrtilla about the teaching opportunity in Mississippi. *Courtesy of New England Historical and Genealogical Society.*

know of her availability should he become aware of any open jobs outside the area. She made it clear that she was willing to travel.

In the early summer of 1846, Fowle wrote to Myrtilla and asked if she would be willing to consider a teaching position in what he called the "South West." He informed her that he had been contacted by a gentleman some weeks earlier who was seeking a teacher and a first assistant in a Southern female institute. The job, he wrote, required an understanding of "the higher English branches and . . . something of French and a touch of music," and paid a salary of $500 a year plus room, board, and travel expenses. He thought the details were "uncommonly favorable" for Myrtilla, though she would have to decide quickly since the new term was set to begin in less than a month. "I have no one in mind but you," he wrote, "and I think you told me you were equal to all he requires."

Fowle's upbeat letter concluded with a kind of warning. In their correspondence Myrtilla had given him the impression that she was supportive of the reform movements of the day and against the institution of slavery. "I have a sort of NOTION that you are an <u>Abolitionist</u>," he wrote. This statement was, in fact, an ominous reference to Southern attitudes on the issue of slavery.

Northern abolitionists were viewed by many Southerners as arrogant troublemakers who interfered with matters beyond their own states and interests. It was, indeed, dangerous at the time for an outspoken Northerner to express his or her abolitionist views in the Southern states. Slavery, and the workforce it provided, was an important and, in the view of some, a necessary part of the Southern economy. At the time, public schools in the South were almost nonexistent. Qualified teachers were in great demand for private schools and plantations, but parents and school directors worried about antislavery views of teachers from the North. The usual Southern opinion of Northern meddlers (as they were viewed) was, "Mind your own business!"

There was tremendous anger and division on both sides of the issue, and Fowle wanted to be sure that Myrtilla would not add to that tension by bringing progressive views to an area of the country that would not be open to them. Myrtilla was certainly against slavery—as was Fowle—but she was definitely not yet a *crusader* on the subject like so many others. For a time, she had even mildly favored a plan to send formerly enslaved people back to Africa. There is no doubt that in 1846 her views on the subject were still in the developing stages. Working in the South, she hoped, would give her a better understanding of the issue and how it must be resolved. She thus assured Fowle that her feelings on the subject of slavery would not interfere with the offered job, and she accepted the position.

Myrtilla's offer of employment had come from Dr. David L. Phares, a good-natured and educated man from Wilkinson

County, Mississippi. Dr. Phares, who was also a prominent scientist, educator, and medical doctor, had in 1842 founded the Newton Female Institute on his 1,200-acre cotton farm in Whitesville, Mississippi. Phares had recently heard William Fowle speak on the subject of geography, and the two had struck up a friendship. Phares hired Myrtilla to teach at the Newton Female Institute.

No sooner had Myrtilla begun preparing for her journey south than word came from Dr. Phares that there had been a delay in starting the current term and that her services were not yet required. She had already quit her job in Providence and had gone into further debt purchasing a new wardrobe for the Southern climate and style. Having no other alternative, she returned the clothing and moved back to upstate New York.

As she patiently waited for her opportunity to teach at the Newton Female Institute, her opinions on women's rights and other reform movements sharpened, and she began reading and sharing books on these subjects. War with Mexico had broken out, and the United States found itself further divided on whether slavery should be permitted to expand into the western territories. Many reformers like Myrtilla raised their voices in opposition to "that abominable war," as one of her friends called it.

Myrtilla became even more vocal in her feminist views. She had always believed that the most powerful weapon available to women was the pen and that the best way to reach the public with social grievances was to write. Early in 1847 she submitted an article for publication to a popular women's magazine, *The Ladies' Wreath*. The editor dismissed Myrtilla's views as "slightly controversial" and refused to publish the article. Then, like so many others who disagreed with Myrtilla's liberal opinions on women's issues, the editor lectured her not to encourage some "vain dream of social equality which will never be realized."

The Seneca Falls Convention of the following year, however, would thrust the struggle of women to the forefront of American culture and become the launch point of the equal rights movement.

———•••———

It had been nearly six months since Myrtilla had heard from Dr. Phares, and she was beginning to lose faith that she ever would. By February 1847, however, he had re-extended his invitation to teach at his school in Mississippi. She was overcome with excitement and made frantic preparations for her new adventure. She had "every thing to think of and almost every thing to do," she wrote to a friend. A month later, Myrtilla boarded a large ship with passage paid by the Newton Female Institute and made the weeklong ocean journey to the connecting hub of New Orleans.

To Myrtilla, who had never traveled south of New York, the strange sights of the Louisiana port city must have been shocking. New Orleans was a confused jumble of commercial wonders; an exotic blend of wealth, decadence, and culture—and all of it tainted by the horrors of human bondage. Slaves, bought and sold like livestock, were paraded through the city streets and corralled in shackles into pens for auction. The cotton industry—the economic engine of the South—was fueled with the forced labor of enslaved people, and their value to some wealthy plantation owners was as important as the crop itself. The stated and heavily enforced law of Louisiana defined in heartbreaking precision the legal status of the African slave:

> A slave is one who is in the power of a master to whom he belongs. The master may sell him, dispose of his person, his industry and his labor: he can do nothing, possess

Seneca Falls Convention

In the early decades of the 19th century, a movement to expand women's rights began to take hold in the United States. At the time, American society was almost completely male dominated, and women had very few legal privileges beyond the family unit. Dissatisfied with this state of affairs, a group of reform-minded women and men began arguing for greater political and social powers to be granted to women. Activists such as Lucretia Mott and Elizabeth Cady Stanton became leaders of this movement and in July 1848 held a well-organized two-day convention in Seneca Falls, New York, that focused the world's attention on the plight of women in society. The Seneca Falls Convention became widely known as the first serious step of the women's rights movement. One of the most important moments of the convention was the adoption by its members of a list of demands, grievances, and positions called the Declaration of Sentiments. The declaration's format clearly and purposefully followed that of America's Declaration of Independence. The authors of both documents sought to communicate a sense of oppression at the hand of tyranny. The Declaration of Sentiments conveyed this sense explicitly by using forceful and compelling language and also implicitly by utilizing Thomas Jefferson's unmistakable style and format. In so doing, the writers of the Seneca Falls declaration effectively declared a moral equivalence between their struggle for equal rights and America's fight for independence from Great Britain. They sent a message of suffering, oppression, and *revolution*.

nothing, nor acquire anything but what must belong to the master.

Fifteen years before Myrtilla's trip, a young hired hand by the name of Abraham Lincoln witnessed for the first time a slave auction in New Orleans. "A vigorous and comely mulatto girl was being sold," related one historian.

She underwent a thorough examination at the hands of the bidders; they pinched her flesh and made her trot up and down the room like a horse, to show how she moved, and in order, as the auctioneer said, that "bidders might satisfy themselves" whether the article they were offering to buy was sound or not.

Lincoln reportedly flinched with revulsion and quickly left the scene in disgust. "I can say, knowing it," remarked one of Lincoln's comrades, "that it was on this trip that he formed his opinions of slavery. It run its iron in him then and there."

William Fowle had promised Myrtilla that her journey would steer her "beyond all reach of the sickly regions." Perhaps he had never been to New Orleans. Anxious to leave the city, she boarded a steamboat for the 135-mile trip north on the mighty Mississippi River to Fort Adams, Mississippi, just over the Louisiana border. As she passed the attractive and sturdy towns dotting the shores of the meandering river, Myrtilla no doubt relaxed and thought about the road ahead.

The Newton Female Institute was once described as "a finishing school for the daughters of the well-to-do." The school provided education for the children of wealthy landowners who lived on lavish cotton plantations, some of which were operated through the sweat and labor of enslaved African Americans.

Wilkinson County was located on the southwesternmost corner of the state, about 30 miles east of Fort Adams on the Mississippi River; the county enslaved more African Americans than virtually any other county in the state. Myrtilla soon witnessed that reality firsthand.

In published advertisements, Dr. Phares boasted that his institute "is not surpassed by any in the South for health and morality." In what should have been a hint to Myrtilla of what was expected of her, Phares stated that "the Trustees of the Institute will secure the services of the best teachers whom they can employ. . . . It will be attempted to elevate the standard of female education. All the faculties, physical, intellectual, and moral will be so trained as to render the pupil an ornament to the best society, and useful to her fellow beings." Among the strict set of rules that the students were expected to follow was found the following: "It is desirable that every pupil practice the precepts and principles of the New Testament."

Myrtilla quickly adjusted to her duties at the Newton Female Institute, and though she found Dr. Phares's wife to be a mean and unhappy woman, she enjoyed a good working relationship with the doctor himself. She came to admire and respect him for his strong character and integrity, but there was one major problem—Dr. Phares was a slaveholder.

Myrtilla was deeply troubled by this hypocrisy: Dr. Phares required his teachers and students to show strong moral character while he himself forced enslaved people to work on the very grounds where those teachers served and those students learned. Her anger soon intensified as she began exploring the region on her days off, witnessing slavery and its effects in the towns of Wilkinson County and beyond. "The sound of the lash was wafted to her ears in the dim watches of the night," wrote Ellen O'Connor. "The slaves herded and fed like beasts

Gordon, a man who
escaped slavery in
Mississippi, bears the
scars that he received
from numerous
whippings. *Courtesy of
National Portrait Gallery,
Smithsonian Institution;
Photograph by McPherson and
Oliver*

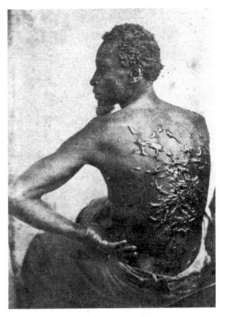

. . . subjected to the unre-
strained passions of bru-
tal masters,—all this was
exposed to her in its star-
tling hideousness." The
sights were far worse than Myrtilla had read about while in the
North. They disgusted her and made her physically ill.

Though she did not at first speak of her anguish, she wrote
home to friends and family about the horrors she saw. She
described Southern culture and the social effects of slavery upon
both black and white people, males and females. The "unjust,
unnatural, and barbarous" system of slavery, she believed, was
filled with "unmitigated evil to all classes and sexes." As harmful as slavery was to its immediate victims—African Americans—Myrtilla noted that slavery might be just as harmful to
white slaveholders and their children. Southerners had become
so accustomed to the institution as an everyday part of life
that they did not see African Americans as people. Slaves were
treated as animals rather than human beings, and that treatment degraded both blacks and whites. Even Dr. Phares, an
otherwise good and decent man, had seemingly lost his sense

of humanity in his efforts to follow Southern customs. His own children, who were also Myrtilla's students, had grown up with the reality of human bondage and had accepted it as commonplace. She did her best to delicately teach her students that all human beings were entitled to dignity and justice regardless of their color. One friend from home, upon learning of the conditions Myrtilla was witnessing, advised her, "In heaven's name my dear Myrtle, do all the good you can; let your light shine and sweet peace of conscience shall be yours with your heavenly father's blessing. Would that you could teach the <u>black</u> children of our Love as well as his <u>white</u> ones."

Feeling helpless to change the system but ashamed if she did not at least try, Myrtilla decided that she must speak with Dr. Phares about her feelings. The situation was taking a physical toll on her, and her health was beginning to fail again.

One afternoon in the sultry heat of the Mississippi summer, Myrtilla nervously approached Dr. Phares and asked if she might have a word. She openly confessed her "mental sufferings" over slavery and explained her moral objections to the treatment of African Americans as mere property. Expecting to be fired on the spot, and perhaps hoping for it, she asked permission to leave for home.

To her total relief and surprise, Dr. Phares agreed with her views on slavery, and the two began a lively discussion on the subject. An educated and rational man, Phares informed Myrtilla that he felt no different about the system of Southern slavery than she did. He was uncomfortable with being a slaveholder himself but treated those he enslaved as well as could be expected, he said. When she begged him to release the people he held in bondage, Phares sadly said that it was out of his power to do so. Without a workforce of enslaved laborers, he could not afford to keep his cotton farm going while his competition freely used slave labor. The workers must be forced to work against their will or the entire economy of the South would suffer, he told her. Similar to many other Southern slaveholders, Phares no doubt rationalized that his slaves fared better in captivity than they would if he set them free. "They are but grown up children," he told Myrtilla with tears in his eyes.

Myrtilla was comforted to learn of Dr. Phares's opposition to slavery even though she believed that he contributed to the problem by being a slaveholder himself. She now felt that she had a friend in him and that she wasn't alone in her hatred of slavery. She decided to remain in Mississippi for the time being and quietly do what she could, though she was still terribly upset by the Southern culture that seemed to embrace the institution. In the coming weeks, the two had more "calm, penetrating discussions" as she called them, and the more they spoke the more Myrtilla's sense of outrage sharpened.

Founder of the Newton Female Institute and a slaveholder himself, David Lewis Phares helped to shape Myrtilla's goals as an educator of African Americans. *Courtesy of David L. Phares Collection, Manuscripts Division, Mississippi State University Libraries*

Though a mutual respect had developed between the two, Phares had risked much in keeping Myrtilla as a teacher at his school. Had Myrtilla's deep-seated antislavery leanings been known to the slaveholding parents and supporters of the institute, Phares's teaching career in Mississippi could very likely have ended. Clearly he valued Myrtilla's work and sympathized with her opinions.

The injustice of slavery continued to take a deep toll on Myrtilla. She lost her appetite and found herself crying day and night. Her strength wasted away, and soon she became sick to the point where she found it difficult to teach. "Wherever I go, horror and despair attend me and I do not wish to become any more acquainted with a people who shock me by their injustice," she informed Dr. Phares in a letter that July as he traveled in the North. "The more I know the more I hate!" She begged him to send her home, but he would not hear of it. She would have no choice but to fight through her pain and grief and continue her appointed work.

Upon his return home from the North, Dr. Phares revealed to Myrtilla that he had been thinking about a sweeping plan of gradual emancipation, or freedom, for all people enslaved in the South. Since the overriding reason for slavery was economic, Phares contemplated raising private money for the outright *purchase* of slaves from their masters. "If properly managed," he wrote, "it will . . . enable them in a few years to shake the whole existing system of slavery from its rotten foundation leaving it to live only in the history of things past." Though many people in the North would reject such a plan as being impractical and unacceptably slow in its results, Myrtilla agreed with the gradual approach to emancipation. She felt that it was the only practical way to end slavery. She embraced Dr. Phares's idea and began thinking about how she might personally add to its success.

During one conversation with Dr. Phares, Myrtilla suggested that, at the very least, enslaved people should be "properly instructed"—that they should receive some level of education. At that moment, inspiration overtook her, and she peered earnestly into Dr. Phares's eyes. Why, she excitedly asked, could she not teach the workers on his farm? He replied that it was illegal in Mississippi to teach slaves; if they attempted to do so, they risked fine, imprisonment, or worse. He no doubt reminded her that many enslaved people had been whipped or branded or had fingers removed for the crime of being caught with a book. Phares thought for a moment, then calmly told her that many in the South doubted the sincerity of Northern abolitionists and those who supported them. African American men, women, and children in the North still suffered from hatred and discrimination, so why, suggested Phares, should not the work to educate "them first" be undertaken before demanding that the slaveholding South take the same measure? True sincerity of cause would require the North to act on its own before demanding that the South do so.

"In that hour," later wrote Myrtilla, "I resolved to open a normal school for Colored youth."

"THE ANTISLAVERY ALTAR OF MY COUNTRY"

By the spring of 1848, it was entirely clear to Myrtilla that she would be unable to bring about the social changes she desired while working in Mississippi. Dr. Phares's plan to gradually purchase the emancipation of Southern slaves had fallen upon deaf ears, as had her consequent scheme to educate them. Angered to learn that teaching African American children in the South was illegal, she became frustrated and disillusioned with her job and finally decided to leave the area. "The truth is," she wrote to Dr. Phares, "there is so much meanness here, the more anyone breaks their neck to do good, the more are they hated."

Myrtilla *had* tried to do good in Mississippi. Months earlier she had sent a written copy of Dr. Phares's plan to Gerrit Smith with an emotional plea for his assistance, only to be told that he could not agree to a plan that tolerated even one more day of slavery. As a friend of the Underground Railroad in New York State, Smith would soon be supporting a daring scheme for the mass escape of enslaved people from Washington, DC. A *gradual* resolution of problems, as Myrtilla now learned, was not in the cards for Gerrit Smith. He counseled her that "immediate unconditional emancipation is a more excellent way."

And on New Year's Day 1848, a day of deep reflection for Myrtilla, she once again wrote to her old friend and correspondent William Seward, who had returned to his job as a lawyer since ending his term as governor of New York. "I address you, Sir," wrote Myrtilla, "because I deem you more intelligent on the subject of American Slavery than many others." She also enclosed a written statement of Dr. Phares's plan of emancipation and made a passionate argument for a gradual approach to the issue of slavery. According to Myrtilla, immediate emancipation, as many in the North supported, was totally impractical and would never be granted. Dr. Phares's plan, she reasoned, "may be accomplished surely and nobly by a <u>union</u> of forces." Myrtilla's letter, she later found out, never reached Seward, but it demonstrated her heartfelt yet thoughtful position on the abolition of slavery.

From Mississippi came the great calling of Myrtilla's life, but also a heartache that she had never known before—a heartache that would weigh heavily on her mind and body. As she thought about the evils of slavery and the unrighteousness of the people who supported it, the influence of the institution settled upon her "like a great grief which could not be removed as long as the cause existed." It was, she wrote, "an agony inexpressible."

She had stayed nearly two years in the toxic environment of slavery—a tribute to her own persistent abilities—but now, unable to sleep, losing weight, and fighting illness, Myrtilla parted ways with Dr. Phares and the Newton Female Institute. She described herself at that time as "a miserable skeleton" waiting for death. Ellen O'Connor wrote, "At last, the combined moral, mental, and physical strain was too much. Her health

utterly gave way, and she was sent home, apparently to die."
Myrtilla had suffered with poor health for most of her life, but when she returned to her father's cottage in Madison County, New York, in June 1848, her friends and family were startled by her frail and sickly appearance and feared that, this time, she might not recover. Still suffering from chronic tuberculosis and complications of her ongoing spinal ailment, Myrtilla solemnly vowed, should she be allowed to live, to devote her remaining days "to the elevation and welfare of the enslaved race." With renewed determination, she slowly began to recover her health, and within several months of leaving the South her vitality had somewhat improved.

----◆----

Perhaps as a result of a new spiritual trend that had spread across the "Burned-Over District" of central and western New York State in the early 19th century, reform movements such as feminism and abolitionism had found a home in the region. Progressive-minded citizens of the area and supporters of the Underground Railroad demanded the emancipation of all enslaved people and created, in 1835, their firebrand organization, the New York State Antislavery Society. In 1848 the Seneca Falls Convention inspired a groundbreaking examination of women's rights. Leaders of these causes, such as William R. Smith, William Chaplin, and Gerrit Smith, often met in homes and churches around the state, planning their tactics and defending against the brutal criticisms that would surely follow.

Myrtilla saw a clear connection between the reformist battles of the abolitionist and feminist movements. "The condition of women and slaves are not without a parallel, and she may not hope for emancipation until the grosser form of . . . slavery

Burned-Over District

Born in the western region of New York, a mindset of religious, social, and cultural reform swept across much of the northeastern United States beginning in the late 1820s. That region of New York was nicknamed the "Burned-Over District" by a Presbyterian minister. Borrowed from a symbolic forest fire or inferno, the term *Burned-Over District* refers to the sweeping and all-encompassing influence of religious fervor. From village to village, a wave of spiritual revival spread across the countryside, and new sects and religious beliefs began to take root. Not only did the progressive movements of women's rights and abolitionism find homes in the Burned-Over District, but also new homespun religions and spiritual cults came to life among the simple, self-taught inhabitants of the region. From this small area of New York, many "end-of-the-world" belief systems evolved, and some well-known and established religions that survive even today, such as the Church of Jesus Christ of Latter-Day Saints, Jehovah's Witnesses, and the Seventh-Day Adventist Church, found their origin in the region. Beyond the development of formal religions and sects, the Burned-Over District was also home to a spiritual movement focused on mystical healing, trances, and contact with the dead—a movement that would be followed and advocated by Myrtilla Miner.

shall be passed away," wrote one observer. In Myrtilla's view it was only natural for a feminist to despise discrimination of any kind and in all its forms. And she took the argument a step further. "The celebration of Independence," she wrote one Fourth of July, ". . . has stirred deep emotions in my soul. . . . In the Constitution I have found nothing to prompt a spirit of patriotic action, on the part of any save 'white male citizens.'" Women, concluded Myrtilla after a study of the founding documents, were "left to the same degraded position in regard to liberty as the degraded African."

Myrtilla's personal beliefs on the subject of abolition were, as demonstrated in her letters to Gerrit Smith and William Seward, a little more complex. Even among those who wanted freedom for enslaved people, opinions differed as to how that freedom should be achieved. Many, like Smith, took the rigid (and at the time, radical) position in favor of immediate emancipation. Not another day of human bondage was acceptable to the followers of this view. Others, Myrtilla included, believed that no matter how strongly slavery was hated, immediatism, as it was called, was impractical and would never be granted. "The safety of the country," wrote Myrtilla of abolition, "requires that it be gradual."

As she recovered from her illness back home in New York, she debated issues such as these in meetings with other like-minded thinkers of the day. In the Farmington, New York, home of William R. Smith, an abolitionist Quaker who had helped organize the New York State Antislavery Society, Myrtilla was introduced to Underground Railroad activists such as William Chaplin and Smith's father, Asa B. Smith. One evening in the winter of 1849, the subject of black education arose, and Asa suggested the possibility of at some point establishing a "colored school" in Washington, DC. Aware of Myrtilla's notable teaching experiences, he asked whether she would be willing to take

Immediatism vs. Gradualism

Though all abolitionists opposed slavery in every form, they debated different philosophies as to exactly how to abolish it prior to the Civil War. Some people believed in the concept of immediatism, the idea that slavery was a sin and must therefore be ended immediately, without compromise or delay. This religious approach, championed by the outspoken abolitionist publisher William Lloyd Garrison, was first advanced in Great Britain as a response to Parliament's slow action in abolishing slavery in the West Indies; the idea arrived in the United States by the late 1820s. Promoters of immediatism believed that nothing short of the unconditional, immediate abolition of all slavery was required. The cultural and economic reality of the slaveholding states, however, caused many abolitionists to conclude that immediatism was simply impractical and unachievable. This other group favored gradualism, a cautious approach to ending slavery that took into consideration the vast economic impact on the South that abolition would cause.

charge of such a school when the time came. Though she had resolved to teach African American children and was convinced of the rightness of the cause, Myrtilla did not consider herself yet sufficiently recovered from her illness "to undertake so vast a work." The actual details of her mission had never been settled in her mind, and her financial situation was still bleak. Thus, when confronted with the question, she hesitated. "I could give no satisfactory reply at that time," she later wrote. She could not undertake the momentous task of establishing a school for black children in antebellum (pre–Civil War) America without a great deal of mental preparation and soul-searching. But, in addition to her poor health, she suffered from the very human trait of procrastination, and at times she lacked direction. She would grow weary of projects and quickly "dart off in another tangent," as one friend observed upon Myrtilla's glib suggestion that she might go into medicine. Indeed, her letters reveal that at one point she even considered missionary work in China. "What shall we hear of you next . . . ," asked her friend, "that you are going to join the army?"

In August 1849, Myrtilla accepted a teaching position at the newly established Friendship Academy in Allegany County, New York, at a salary of $250 per year with the goal of improving her financial situation. Her brother Isaac had for some time been coaxing her to take the job and was quite relieved to see her settle in Friendship, a town close to his new home. Her younger sister Achsa, always wishing to please her elder sibling, had earlier taught at a school in Friendship and was now attending the Clover Street Seminary in Rochester, upon Myrtilla's urging. With their father unsupportive of Achsa's further education, Myrtilla took on the financial burden of her sister's tuition. As poor as Myrtilla may have been, she always provided money and assistance for her little sister.

Myrtilla's relationship with Achsa was somewhat complicated. Achsa always wanted to please her older sister yet often fell short. They looked and sounded very much alike, but with similarity sometimes came friction. "There was a spirit of intense interest each for the other; sometimes, in each, a tenseness," wrote one historian. When Achsa at one point decided to forego school-teaching in favor of embroidery instruction, Myrtilla became very angry. Dismissively informing Achsa that she might do as she pleased, Myrtilla left no doubt about her disapproval and scolded Achsa for not recognizing the value of her guidance.

"I think you misjudge me," responded Achsa, "for I certainly do appreciate your kindness and have said repeatedly that you exerted yourself more on my account than any other person living. If I have seemed ungrateful do forgive it." Myrtilla hoped her sister would excel in the teaching field and was bitterly disappointed if that goal seemed to waver in any fashion. She loved Achsa but expected the highest standard of excellence from her—a standard that her sister sometimes grew weary of. "Perhaps you think I love you best when you are farthest off," wrote Achsa. Nonetheless, Myrtilla would soon have great plans for her younger sister.

Myrtilla's time in the town of Friendship was short and chaotic. She got into a dispute with the school principal, who had chosen to employ his personal friends as teachers, leaving Myrtilla with reduced privileges and activities. When she objected, the principal dismissed her. An appeal to the school directors did not help, and so again she was left without a job or money to support herself, much less the means to cover the costs of Achsa's education. "If you are not going to teach there, I would give my whole interest in the gold mines of California," wrote Achsa in joking reference to the Gold Rush—the westward clamor for riches that had begun at Sutter's Mill the year before.

As Myrtilla's arrangements at the Friendship Academy unraveled, her thoughts of bringing education to African Americans once again began to grow. Intrigued by Asa B. Smith's suggestion to establish a "colored school" in Washington, DC, and encouraged by her own recovering health, she began to seriously consider the idea. She sent Achsa to study in Providence, Rhode Island, under the care of the Atwater cousins, as she herself had done, with the main goal of obtaining further instruction in music and the arts, two areas in which Myrtilla did not consider herself skilled. Achsa would now play a vital role in Myrtilla's design; she would join her sister in the nation's capital and assist her in the great plan to bring education to the black population. "I am quite willing to go to Washington as you propose if it is best," wrote Achsa. Understanding the dangers of such a plan, however, Achsa quickly added, "I am not sure I would put down my cautiousness enough to undertake the unreasonable."

In February 1850, Myrtilla again wrote to Gerrit Smith, informing him that she had returned from Mississippi and that she and her sister were now ready to travel to Washington, DC, to put her plan into action.

Now, sir, it is in regard to establishing a school for colored people in the City of Washington that I address you. . . . If the leading abolitionists in our country deem such a step desirable, I offer myself on the altar for teacher. No man can fill the station, because <u>men</u> may be attacked by men and driven from their posts, but a woman claims lenity from her weakness and may not be harmed. Few women would willingly throw themselves into a situation where so much opposition and disgrace must be met from the populace, but this I mind not, having lived too long to deem it injurious. My hand trembles and refuses to serve me well as I here transcribe the offering I make of <u>myself</u> upon the Antislavery Altar of my country.

The critical issue of American slavery had found its way into the halls of Congress by 1850. For the previous four years, slavery had been the subject of vigorous debate among US senators and congressmen. The Wilmot Proviso, a measure that attempted to forbid the spread of slavery into the newly acquired territories from the Mexican War, had been proposed and reproposed on various occasions but each time had been rejected by the Senate.

The boundary line between slaveholding and free territories was fiercely disputed, and the status of California, which sought to enter the Union as a free state, was pushed and pulled in a political tug-of-war. Finally, in January 1850, Kentucky senator Henry Clay introduced a series of resolutions that would become the Compromise of 1850 and temporarily avert a crisis between the North and South. In return for Southern concessions, however, the Fugitive Slave Act was passed, providing broad powers and harsh punishments in the search for runaway slaves. "No measure for the security of slavery ever roused deeper indignation," wrote Ellen O'Connor. As part of the compromise, the sale of enslaved people, though not slavery as an institution, would be abolished in the nation's capital. To Southern slaveholders, it was merely the first step in what they viewed as a Northern-driven plot to end slavery itself.

On July 9, during the debates for the Compromise of 1850, the president of the United States, Zachary Taylor, died from complications of food poisoning. His death paved the way for his more compromise-driven successor, Millard Fillmore, to advance the legislation. Within mere weeks, however, another death would shake Myrtilla Miner to the core.

Wilmot Proviso

The Mexican War, which began in 1846, resulted in the US conquest of the territories now comprising California, Utah, Nevada, Arizona, and New Mexico. With the acquisition of these lands, and considering the strong American ambition toward westward expansion in general, the thorny and complicated question of whether slavery should be permitted in those territories became the predominant political issue of the day. In August 1846 President James K. Polk requested $2 million from Congress to be used for the ultimate settlement of the war and the development of a treaty with Mexico. Concerned that the new territories would be admitted into the United States as slaveholding states, a Pennsylvania congressman named David Wilmot submitted an amendment to President Polk's expenditure bill proposing that slavery be prohibited in any territories acquired from Mexico as a result of the war. The amendment, ultimately named the Wilmot Proviso, passed in the House of Representatives but was blocked in the proslavery Senate. The issue reappeared during later congressional sessions but was voted down on each occasion, leaving open for future resolution the question of slavery in the western territories. Although the Wilmot Proviso would never be enacted into law, it highlighted the growing tension between North and South over slavery and signaled the start of a fiery political debate that ultimately led to the Civil War.

The Compromise of 1850 and the Fugitive Slave Act

In December 1849, following the Mexican War, California asked to be admitted to the United States as a free, nonslave state. At the time, divisions over slavery in the expanding country were causing fierce arguments and growing regional tensions. In an effort to prevent a crisis over the issue, Senator Henry Clay from Kentucky introduced a series of measures to strike a compromise between the two sides. After a contentious debate led by Senators Stephen Douglas and Daniel Webster, five separate bills were agreed upon that provided enough enticement to each side to temporarily settle the issue. The Compromise of 1850, as it became known, admitted California into the Union as a free state; settled the border lines of Texas; recognized the territories of Utah and New Mexico, where the people would decide by popular vote whether to allow or abolish slavery; abolished the slave trade (but not slavery itself) in Washington, DC; and strengthened the Fugitive Slave Act. Of all the measures agreed to in the Compromise of 1850, the Fugitive Slave Act proved to be most controversial and problematic. The act required, under threat of fine or imprisonment, that state officials and private citizens, whether from free or slave states, aid in the capture and return of any runaway slave. It was now a crime for anyone in the North to harbor a person fleeing slavery or provide that person with aid. The Fugitive Slave Act galvanized the antislavery coalition like no other force.

"I am now sitting in the sick room of our beloved Achsa," wrote a member of the Atwater family to Myrtilla on July 21 from Providence, "and while she is quite free from suffering we think she cannot live many hours." An infection of the lower intestine had recently sickened her and a "sudden and unexpected change" brought alarm and then sad resignation to the family. Achsa died later that day.

When word reached Myrtilla that her younger sister had passed away, she was overcome with what she later described as a "choking grief . . . and intense pain," an "inexpressible agony." The drive, the zeal that typified Myrtilla now seemed to leave her. Just as her dreams of working together with her sister toward a great and principled goal appeared to be moving forward, word of Achsa's death seemed to change everything. "I half think I will return to Providence . . . and stay there as long as I live and die as soon as I can," she wrote to a friend.

In the weeks and months that followed, Myrtilla remained heartbroken, alone, and virtually penniless. In what would begin a lifelong obsession with spiritualism, one of many philosophical movements to sweep across New York State in the 1840s and '50s, Myrtilla attempted to make contact with the spirit of her dead sister through a series of séances and spiritual consultations. She seemed to be searching for a higher meaning of life through exploration of the supernatural world, and in a sense, Achsa's death prompted Myrtilla to look beyond her daily problems and into the depths of her own heart. Finally understanding life's shortness and uncertainty, she came out of her despair and began thinking again of the hardship of others and her plans for the future.

Myrtilla had been disappointed to receive no response from Gerrit Smith to her offer earlier in the year to open a school for black children in Washington, DC. Smith, a prominent voice for many progressive causes, was besieged with numerous proposals and appeals from a variety of concerned citizens. He was an advocate for the immediate emancipation of enslaved people and had rejected Dr. Phares's plan to purchase their freedom because it was too gradual an approach. He now viewed Myrtilla's decision to educate African Americans in much the same way. Educating black people, he concluded, would not bring an end to slavery.

By the spring of 1850, having received no support or direction from Smith or his abolitionist colleagues, Myrtilla was forced to accept a teaching position at the Smethport Academy in McKean County, Pennsylvania. Her abysmal financial situation required that she work. Here, undaunted, she continued to develop plans to open her own school. Her unselfish character and

Gerrit Smith, abolitionist, philanthropist, and staunch advocate for the antislavery cause. He corresponded with Myrtilla about plans for her school but ultimately offered little support. *Brady-Handy Collection, Prints & Photographs Division, Library of Congress, LC-DIG-cwpbh-02631*

interest in humanity led her to visit prisoners in the county jail at Smethport, to sing to them and bring them comfort. Her students soon came to understand the strict yet unique and principled nature of their instructor. "As the time passed on," wrote one pupil, "we saw embodied in our teacher a character entirely original and independent in its relations to human judgments and worldly considerations, but grandly responsive to any demands that were made by human needs, and to all commands that were recognized as coming from the Father of All."

It was clear by now that Myrtilla would receive little guidance from the leaders of the abolitionist movement in her mission to open a school. Throughout 1850 she personally conducted careful research and analysis into African American education. Her decision to establish a school in the nation's capital was not made simply at the suggestion of Asa B. Smith, nor was it made in one day. The proper location of the school was a matter of great consequence, and Myrtilla studied the question in detail. As late as July 1850 she had still not completely settled upon Washington, DC, as the definite site. She had warned Gerrit Smith that her dwindling finances might even force her to accept another teaching job in what she called the "slavocracy" of the Deep South, but careful study and good sense kept her from doing so.

In researching locations, she learned, first and foremost, that unlike many Southern states, Washington, DC, had no specific laws against the education of free African Americans. In 1804 the city had adopted a law that established public schools. While the actual wording of the law did not specifically exclude black children from these schools, the unwritten law did. Public schools were fully segregated, and attempts to create privately funded black schools were generally opposed by much of the white population, though not legally forbidden. Myrtilla recognized that many people would strongly oppose her idea—but that the law itself did not prohibit it.

Though the Compromise of 1850 had ended the slave trade in Washington, DC, slavery itself continued. "Gangs of slaves, handcuffed together, to be sent for sale further South, passed under the shadow of the Capitol," wrote Ellen O'Connor, "and there was a slave pen, with its whipping-post, across the river at Alexandria. It was a crime to teach these slaves to read."

But not all black people were enslaved. Many were purchased by abolitionists from their enslavers with the aim of releasing them from bondage, and some were granted their freedom by their masters. In her research, Myrtilla learned that over 8,000 free African Americans, some formerly enslaved and others born in freedom, resided in Washington, DC, in 1850, about 2,000 of whom were children. Further, the city contained the greatest number of untaught black residents of any city that did not prohibit black education. The nation's capital, she soon concluded, was the best location for her experiment. She could not educate the people still held in bondage, but she would turn her attention to those she could legally teach.

Of equal importance to her decision to locate her school in Washington, DC, Myrtilla felt it her Christian duty to assist those she referred to as "sufferers in this guilty city." Without proper instruction, she reasoned, black women in Washington were subjected to "great temptations to evil" more so than elsewhere, and she believed they were particularly entitled to Christian goodwill. Also, Myrtilla knew that many of her political allies in Washington, even some members of Congress, would be close by and perhaps willing to aid her. Finally, the symbolism and cultural significance of establishing her school in the heart of the nation's capital as an example to the rest of the country was, no doubt, too appealing to pass up. "If an influence can be felt in behalf of the colored people anywhere," she wrote, "it can be most felt in the City of Washington."

She once again wrote to William Seward, who was now a US senator, and requested his opinion of her idea. Seward had proven to be a trusted confidant and, in Myrtilla's eyes, a "friend to humanity." He had supported her in the fight for women's rights, and she had faith in his opinions on political and cultural matters. She explained that her life's calling involved the "afflicted... & down-trodden colored race in our own free country," and she asked for his judgment on the establishment of a school for African American girls in Washington, DC. Seward quickly replied that he was unqualified to advise her on such a subject. "Although *in* Washington," he wrote, I am not *of* it."

Ever the optimist, and by this time fully committed to her idea, Myrtilla gleefully responded, thanking Seward for his letter—"that in it was no word of fearful hopeless doubt." Her mind was now made up, and despite the lack of any real support from her abolitionist colleagues, she began to envision a timeframe for her project. She had resolved to travel south to Washington, DC, and establish her school for "colored misses" by the fall of 1851.

"I propose nothing new in principle," she wrote to the famous novelist E.D.E.N. Southworth,

> but only a new mode of acting out an old principle—
> which is that no race or people can ever enjoy their right
> without cultivation—& one of the best methods of secur-
> ing to any oppressed people their God-given—but man-
> prevented rights, is to elevate them. . . . I am more than
> ever convinced that the colored people will never rise
> alone & without aid—after receiving only oppression &
> the resulting degradation for so many generations at our

hands. . . . What can I better do than faithfully instruct them?

Soon her objectives began to crystallize and the exact nature of her mission emerged. "Our intention is to educate a class of teachers, who shall be efficient and exert an influence that in ten years from this may be felt," she wrote that summer to a friend.

"We go forth anticipating vast obstacles & many trials but an intelligent friend in Washington writes, that he thinks we can undisturbedly teach colored children there."

"I SHALL TRY IT!"

By 1850 the issue of slavery was placing a great strain on the United States. The Fugitive Slave Act that forced Northerners to participate in the return of runaway slaves only further polarized an already divided nation. In Congress, angry debates took place to abolish slavery in Washington, DC, and Myrtilla's friend Senator William Seward led the charge.

Efforts to attack the institution of slavery in the South, however, were generally regarded as dangerous and futile. Southern defiance to such efforts was determined and often brutal. In 1831, for instance, the outspoken abolitionist and writer William Lloyd Garrison was jailed in Baltimore for the crime of criticizing a slave ship owner. Slavery, plain and simple, had become part of the makeup of Southern culture, and Southern political and social leaders would do almost anything to preserve it.

Despite the obvious dangers, the brave movement against slavery continued in the North. Myrtilla was now willing to boldly carry that movement into perilous Southern territory.

William Lloyd Garrison

William Lloyd Garrison began his professional career at age 13 as an apprentice editor of a New England newspaper called the *Newburyport Herald*. In the coming years he expanded his political awareness and enhanced his skills as a writer and journalist. At age 24 he was introduced to Benjamin Lundy, a pioneering abolitionist and newspaper editor; Garrison soon became coeditor of Lundy's antislavery newspaper, *The Genius of Universal Emancipation*, located in Baltimore. By 1830 Garrison opened his own newspaper, *The Liberator*, in Boston, where his crusading views against slavery were heard loud and clear. Like many of his day, Garrison's abolitionist opinions evolved over time. He initially believed that the best way to deal with the problem of slavery was to return African Americans to Africa—a position advocated by the American Colonization Society. By the time he founded *The Liberator*, however, he had changed his view and turned into a spokesman for immediatism—the immediate and unconditional end of all slavery. Through his newspaper Garrison became one the country's most radical and outspoken critics of slavery. In 1832 he helped to form the New England Antislavery Society and, a year later, founded the American Antislavery Society. In time he developed the radical belief that the US Constitution was a hopelessly flawed proslavery document and that the only solution was a peaceful division of the Union into two separate countries.

Aware that teaching black children in the South would carry grave risks, she was nonetheless bolstered by an "unyielding will when sure of being right."

———◆◆———

Even after years of teaching, Myrtilla was still virtually penniless and did not have the means to set up and maintain her school. A room or building had to be found and rent would need to be paid. There were books, paper, pencils, and other supplies to be purchased and fuel for heat that had to be secured. On top of that she would need to set up her own room and board and other basics of life—all of which would cost additional money. Myrtilla was aware that African American pupils in Washington, DC, would not be able to pay very much, if any, tuition, but she was otherwise totally naive about the financial requirements of her plan. "I thought a school could be established in Washington as well as in any other city, without money," she wrote. In short, Myrtilla had a dream but very few practical means of turning that dream into reality. The support of others—both financial and emotional—would be critical to her success.

Though she boasted that she could establish her school on "moral courage" alone without the approval of others, she quickly came to understand the practical need for funding and assistance. But almost immediately those whom she turned to for support made very clear the difficulty of her challenge. Some, like Gerrit Smith, took little interest in measures that would not result in the immediate emancipation of enslaved people, while others wanted proof that Myrtilla's plan would work before they offered assistance. And most simply believed the idea of educating African Americans in the nation's capital to be reckless and foolhardy.

E.D.E.N. Southworth, the novelist to whom Myrtilla had written a passionate letter outlining her plans, informed her that several people she had spoken with "think your benevolent scheme utterly impracticable." Although sympathetic to the antislavery cause, Southworth concluded that Myrtilla's scheme could never succeed and suggested that she instead pursue "some practicable road of usefulness and happiness."

Myrtilla had also sent a letter to a free African American teacher in Washington, DC, by the name of John F. Cook asking for advice and encouragement. He could provide neither. "I have to be very particular to do nothing knowingly, that would in the least tend to disturb the public zeal, or bring upon me . . . the indignation of the inhabitants," he wrote. "I must therefore respectfully decline giving you any advice upon the subject, and beg leave to refer you to the white friends of this community. . . . I think the less people of color . . . have to do with [the school's] establishment the better for the object itself, and for you personally."

She sought the guidance of Deacon Oren Sage of Rochester, a beloved church leader and a champion of New York education, but he quickly attacked her plan as "presumptuous in the highest degree." On a suggestion from William Seward, Myrtilla wrote to Gamaliel Bailey, the editor of the antislavery newspaper *The National Era*, for advice. He did not respond. And despite an earlier plea to Gerrit Smith "for the protection of the Abolitionists of our country," no offer of protection ever came. It seemed that Myrtilla was alone in her plan to educate African Americans.

Undeterred, she decided to call on Frederick Douglass, a man who had escaped slavery and become one of the nation's leading antislavery spokesmen. Surely, Myrtilla thought, he would support her endeavor.

Frederick Douglass

Born into slavery in 1818 on the eastern shore of Maryland as Frederick Augustus Washington Bailey, this rebellious and intelligent young man would ultimately escape to freedom and one day become the country's most renowned author and speaker for the abolitionist cause. Early in his life, Frederick understood the importance of education, and he secretly taught himself and other slaves how to read. Angered by the injustice of slavery and yearning for freedom, he vowed to escape. In 1838, at age 20, he concealed his identity, escaped north, and changed his name to Frederick Douglass. A free African American woman named Anna Murray—who later became Frederick's wife—helped with the daring plan. Frederick found work as a laborer and attended anti-slavery meetings. He began to speak about his experiences in bondage, and soon his reputation as an orator grew. He took a job with the Massachusetts Anti-Slavery Society and spoke to crowds across the region. In 1845 he published the first of three autobiographies. After he moved to England to avoid capture as a fugitive slave, a group of American abolitionists officially purchased his freedom from slavery. Released from the worry of arrest, he settled in Rochester, New York, where he opened a newspaper, *The North Star*, dedicated to antislavery stories and causes. Frederick championed not only abolition but also women's rights and the Union cause during the Civil War. For the duration of his life he spoke eloquently of the oppression of African Americans and fought for equal rights for all men and women.

At the time, Frederick operated an abolitionist newspaper in Rochester, New York, called *The North Star*. He intended through his newspaper to bring an African American voice to the antislavery movement and to further inspire abolitionists. On the day of Myrtilla's visit, the stern-faced 32-year-old was busily working on the mailing of his newspaper and hardly noticed when she and two mutual friends arrived at his print shop. "It was my custom to continue my work, no matter who came, and hence I barely looked up to give them welcome," he later wrote.

Myrtilla introduced herself to Frederick and, seeing how busy he was, immediately informed him that she intended to travel to the nation's capital to establish a school for "colored girls." Startled, he stopped his work and looked up in amazement. "A slender, wiry, pale (not over[ly]-healthy), but singularly animated figure was before me," he wrote later. Unsure if Myrtilla was serious in what she had said, he studied her face,

Renowned journalist, author, and orator of the abolitionist cause, Frederick Douglass. *Prints & Photographs Division, Library of Congress, LC-USZ62-15887*

Myrtilla Miner, founder of the School for Colored Girls. *Prints & Photographs Division, Library of Congress,* LC-USZ62-95716

and soon all doubt was removed. "I saw at a glance that the fire of a real enthusiasm lighted her eyes, and the true martyr spirit flamed in her soul."

He was both happy and sad about Myrtilla's plan. The commitment she showed in bringing education to African Americans deeply moved and inspired him, but at the same time he knew how difficult it would be for her to succeed: "Here, I thought, is another enterprise, wild, dangerous, desperate, and impracticable, destined only to bring failure and suffering."

The two talked for a while. Myrtilla was in constant motion, pacing back and forth across the room as she spoke. In an open and sincere tone she claimed that her plan was workable and would succeed. She told him that she had lived among Southern slaveholders and knew the South—and she insisted that she was not afraid of the possibility of violence against her or her school. Frederick countered that others had tried to open similar schools and had failed miserably. "To me, the proposition was reckless, almost to the point of madness," he wrote. "In my [mind], I saw this fragile little woman harassed by the law, insulted in the street, a victim of slaveholding malice, and, possibly beaten down by the mob."

Despite Frederick's stern warnings not to attempt the plan, Myrtilla stood strong in her faith. "My argument made no impression upon the heroic spirit before me," he later wrote. "Her resolution was taken, and was not to be shaken or changed."

"I shall try it!" shouted Myrtilla.

In the late spring of 1851 *The National Era*, a Washington, DC, antislavery newspaper, began carrying a 40-week serial called *Uncle Tom's Cabin*, written by Harriet Beecher Stowe, a New England teacher and abolitionist. The fictionalized story depicted harsh scenes of American slavery, and upon its publication in book form the following year, it became a worldwide sensation. *Uncle Tom's Cabin* thrust the issue of slavery into the national spotlight—and further divided the nation like never before.

Harriet Beecher Stowe, author of *Uncle Tom's Cabin* and an avid supporter of Myrtilla's school. *Prints & Photographs Division, Library of Congress, LC-USZ62-11212*

Harriet Beecher Stowe

One of eleven children, Harriet Beecher Stowe was born on June 14, 1811, in Litchfield, Connecticut, to the Reverend Lyman Beecher and his wife, Roxana Foote Beecher. From an early age, Harriet was exposed to strong religious faith and the importance of education and equal rights. She began her formal schooling at the Litchfield Female Academy and then continued at the Hartford Female Seminary, which was founded by her sister Catharine. Harriet would find her place in the world first as a teacher and ultimately as a writer. In 1832 she moved with her father to Cincinnati, Ohio, where she became involved with various literary societies and began strong associations with those in the abolitionist movement. In 1836 she married Calvin Ellis Stowe, a staunch antislavery advocate and a professor at Lane Theological Seminary. The couple had seven children, one of whom died of cholera as an infant. This devastating loss, coupled with the injustice she felt over the Fugitive Slave Act, inspired Harriet to expose the evils of slavery through her writing. While living in Maine in 1850, she wrote what would become one of the world's most famous novels, *Uncle Tom's Cabin*. The book told a fictional story depicting the horrors of slavery, and it enraged the passions of many across the country. Abraham Lincoln, upon meeting Harriet during the Civil War, reportedly said, "So you are the little woman who wrote the book that started this great war."

Though Harriet would later play an important role in sustaining Myrtilla's school, at the time that *Uncle Tom's Cabin* came into its fame, Myrtilla was at a low point in her efforts to gather support. Despite a public whose sympathies had been aroused by Stowe's story and a will that could not be dampened, Myrtilla's work to obtain assistance for her school had fallen on deaf ears. Almost everybody she approached thought her idea wild and irresponsible. Just when all seemed lost, a friend sent her to Harriet Beecher Stowe's brother—Henry Ward Beecher. His help, wrote Myrtilla, "saved us all from the irrecoverable desolation of complete failure."

A New York minister with a flamboyant and charismatic flair, Henry Ward Beecher had become nationally famous in his own right through his captivating and entertaining sermons. He used his growing popularity to bring voice to the antislavery cause and became one of its most effective and influential leaders. When Myrtilla contacted Henry and told him of her plans, she finally received the response she had hoped for. "The thought is a great one," he told her, "too good to fail for want of means." He promised his valuable assistance and directed her to travel to New England at once to secure books, supplies, and funding from his sources.

But again her efforts were met with disappointment. "The very remembrance of it today is like a troubled dream," Myrtilla later wrote. With Henry's help she set up a meeting with a publishing house in Boston to request a donation of books for her venture but was endlessly interrogated by the company directors about her past experiences and what she knew of Washington, DC, and its citizens. Myrtilla did her best to justify her plans, passionately explaining the need for African American education, but she was met with skeptical glances and pessimistic sighs. Unable to provide adequate assurance that she would be able to even open the school, she was forced to leave Boston empty-handed. Even the influence of Henry Ward Beecher had no effect upon the cynicism of the New England book publisher.

Still, Myrtilla would not quit. From her many appeals for aid she finally received a donation of $100 from Mrs. Ednah Thomas, of Aurora, New York, and a bookseller from New York, A. S. Barnes and Company, graciously sent her a variety of books, magazines, and miscellaneous school supplies. A friend from Washington, DC, suggested that a room might be found for the school in the city and that several students might be willing to attend. Beyond that, she wrote, "no one replied encouragingly." With $100 in her pocket, and a promise of future assistance from Henry, Myrtilla set off into the unknown.

"Impelled by a sense of duty and fitness, painful as it might be, I must go, knowing it to be contrary to all human reason and judgment and all together against the wishes and advice of many friends. Still, nothing less than a faithful trial [can] relieve my burdened mind," Myrtilla wrote.

"NATIONAL ONLY IN NAME"

Washington, DC, in 1851 was an unfriendly home for a Northern abolitionist. The lack of support and encouragement from Myrtilla's friends was, perhaps, less a statement of betrayal than a confirmation of reality. The chances of Myrtilla successfully establishing a school for African American girls in the racially charged environment of the nation's capital were, to most people, unlikely. Frederick Douglass understood the cultural temperament of Washington when he warned Myrtilla of the dangers of her plan. Indeed, he wrote of the city:

> Washington, as compared with many other parts of the country, has been, and still is a most disgraceful and scandalous contradiction to the march of civilization. . . . I have no hesitation in saying that the selection of Washington as the National Capital was one of the greatest mistakes made by the fathers of the Republic. . . . Sandwiched between two of the oldest slave states, each of which was a nursery and a hot-bed of slavery; surrounded

by a people accustomed to look upon the youthful members of a colored man's family as a part of the annual crop
for the market; pervaded by the manners, morals, politics,
and religion peculiar to a slaveholding community, the
inhabitants of the National Capital were, from first to last,
frantically and fanatically sectional. It was southern in all
its sympathies and national only in name. . . . It neither
tolerated freedom of speech nor of the press. Slavery was
its idol, and, like all idol worshippers, its people howled
with rage when this ugly idol was called in question.

A view of Washington, DC, as it appeared at the time of Myrtilla's
arrival in the city. "Washington, as compared with many other parts
of the country, has been, and still is a most disgraceful and scandalous
contradiction to the march of civilization," wrote Frederick Douglass. *Popular Graphic Arts, Prints & Photographs Division, Library of Congress,
LC-USZC4-771*

At the beginning of the 19th century, publicly funded education had become a reality in the nation's capital. Through an 1804 Act of Congress, the children of Washington, DC, were finally given the opportunity to attend schools without paying tuition, as was required at private institutions. It was plainly understood by all that free African American children would not be allowed to attend these public schools—despite the fact that their parents were expected to pay taxes at the same rate as white citizens and their attendance was not specifically excluded under the law.

At the time it was illegal for a person living in slavery to be educated, but free black citizens were not treated much better in Southern society. The stated and enforced law of Washington, DC, in fact *required* racial discrimination against free African Americans. The Black Code of the District of Columbia, composed of 105 provisions, required black residents to be off the streets by 10:00 pm, prohibited them from serving on juries or testifying in court against a white person, banned them from bathing in the Potomac River between 5:00 am and 9:00 pm, and even prohibited them from flying kites at the risk of being publicly whipped. The system seemed to encourage the arrest of African Americans. According to the code, "Every negro and mulatto found residing in the City of Washington . . . who shall not be able to establish his or her title to freedom . . . shall be committed to the jail . . . as absconding slaves." In short, though technically "free," these individuals were given few rights beyond those of their enslaved brothers and sisters.

Despite these restrictions, people of color in Washington, DC, yearned to better their situation through learning. Through the assistance of churches and private organizations, schools for black children began quietly appearing in homes and basements around the city. The first school for the education of African

Americans in Washington, DC, was established in 1807, shortly after the creation of the public school system. The Bell School, as it would come to be known, was founded by three formerly enslaved people, none of whom could read or write but who clearly understood that black people must educate themselves in order to overcome their hardships. The school was taught by a white man named Mr. Lowe. Though it only lasted a few years, the school reopened in 1818 with the assistance of a charitable organization made up of free African Americans. The Bell School lit the spark for black education.

In 1809 a white Englishman, Henry Potter, founded a school for African Americans on the corner of Seventh and F Streets in Washington, DC. Shortly thereafter, Anne Marie Becraft became the first African American woman to establish and teach at a school for black children, located on Capitol Hill. Other schools soon sprang up. In 1810 a "capable, very good and exceedingly intelligent" white Englishwoman named Mary Billings founded the first black school in the Georgetown section of the city. She had originally begun teaching white and black children together but faced so much local opposition that she was forced to open an institute for only black children. Billings's school, which lasted through 1821, became a popular and well-attended learning facility, drawing free black students from across the city. In 1823 an African American man named Henry Smothers built a school for black children on 14th and H Streets in Washington, DC, and taught over 100 students. Later, John W. Prout, an African American and "by far the ablest educator among the people at this time," continued Smothers's work and managed to convert the school into a tuition-free institution through the support of private donations. In 1834 the Smothers School was taken over by a Presbyterian minister named John F. Cook—the same black educator whom Myrtilla would later turn to for help and encouragement. Cook's institution would become one of the largest and best-attended black schools in the city.

Other than Mary Billings's attempt to integrate white and black children in the same school, few of these institutions generated much if any open opposition or hostility in Washington, DC. For the most part these schools were attended by many pupils and only failed, when and if they did, due to lack of money. They were encouraged by antislavery whites who recognized the need to educate African Americans, and they were scorned—but not prevented—by those with a less tolerant view. In 1831, however, this lenience toward black education changed in a radical way.

———•—•———

On February 12, 1831, a total solar eclipse darkened the Virginia sky and seized the attention of bewildered residents. "Every person in the city," wrote a reporter from the *Richmond Enquirer*, "was star gazing, from bleary-eyed old age to the most bright-eyed infancy." To a 31-one-year-old enslaved man named Nat Turner, however, the eclipse was a sign from the heavens that it was time to prepare his plan for action. Turner, like so many of his fellow slaves, had been abused and ill-treated since childhood by his Southern masters, and anger and defiance welled within him.

In the small Southern village called Cross Keys, Virginia, Turner led a two-day slave rebellion beginning on August 21, 1831. The bloody event resulted in the deaths of 55 white citizens.

The black men passed from house to house,—not pausing, not hesitating, as their terrible work went on. . . .

There was no gratuitous outrage beyond the death-blow itself, no insult, no mutilation; but in every house they entered, that blow fell on man, woman, and child,—nothing that had a white skin was spared.

Wild rumors and exaggerated versions of the incident began flying around the state, and when word of the uprising reached the governor, hundreds of local militiamen were dispatched. The response of the white community in Virginia was predictably harsh and appallingly disproportionate. In the name of justice and vengeance, "the white people had commenced the destruction of the negroes." According to one account, "A party

An 1831 depiction of Nat Turner's Rebellion. "Nothing that had a white skin was spared," wrote one journalist. *Prints & Photographs Division, Library of Congress, LC-USZ62-33451*

of horsemen started from Richmond with the intention of killing every colored person they saw in Southampton County. They stopped opposite the cabin of a free colored man, who was hoeing in his little field. They called out, 'Is this Southampton County?' He replied, 'Yes, Sir, you have just crossed the line, by yonder tree.' They shot him dead and rode on."

As retribution for Nat Turner's murderous uprising, hundreds of African Americans, both enslaved and free, were slaughtered without trial and with utter cruelty. The resulting fear and mistrust among white citizens would spread across the country and last for decades.

Amid this backdrop of anger, the black population of Washington, DC, experienced a cooling of any previously enjoyed goodwill from white residents. The city churches began refusing to admit African American families and closed their doors to black schools that had used church buildings. The precarious peace that had previously existed between the races in Washington had sadly ended.

This period of anger and mistrust in the nation's capital reached its peak on a hot summer night in 1835 when an 18-year-old enslaved man named Arthur Bowen supposedly threatened his enslaver with an ax. Anna Maria Thornton, who was the widow of a well-known city architect, claimed that Bowen had entered her bedroom in the night and raised the ax in a menacing way. Though Thornton later changed her story and pleaded for Bowen's pardon, the event caused a storm of rage among the white citizens of Washington, DC.

At the time there were numerous free black residents in the city, and Northern abolitionists had begun actively petitioning for the end of slavery. With the Nat Turner Rebellion fresh in their minds, and feeling threatened by the Arthur Bowen incident, a group of about 300 to 400 drunken laborers in the city set out seeking revenge. They unsuccessfully stormed the jail where Bowen was being held and then turned their fury upon the business of an educated free black man named Beverly Snow. The men ransacked Snow's stylish and highly regarded restaurant and destroyed most of its furniture. When Snow himself couldn't be found, the mob moved on to John Cook's school on the corner of 14th and H Streets and destroyed the books and furnishings and heavily damaged the building. Through the night the "Snow Riot," as it would come to be known, caused fear and havoc among the free black citizens of Washington, DC.

The effects of Nat Turner's Rebellion and the Snow Riot were not confined to the Southern states. When Myrtilla met with Frederick Douglass in 1851, among the stern warnings that he gave her was a reminder of the persecution of Prudence Crandall in the Northern state of Connecticut.

Like Myrtilla, Prudence Crandall was a schoolteacher who had dedicated herself to educating young people. In 1831 she established a private girls' school in Canterbury, Connecticut,

Prudence Crandall, who established a school for African American girls in Canterbury, Connecticut—and was sent to jail for doing so. *Courtesy of the Prudence Crandall Museum, State of Connecticut, Department of Economic and Community Development*

that was supported by the community and recognized as one of the best schools in the state. The school was attended by white girls only.

At the time she settled in Canterbury, Prudence was not familiar with the abolitionist movement, though she had been brought up as a Quaker and believed in the equality of all people regardless of color. In time she learned of the mistreatment of enslaved people, and a sense of moral duty rose within her.

In September 1832, Prudence was approached by a local African American girl named Sarah Harris, who requested admission to Prudence's school. At first Prudence hesitated, fearing that admitting a black student would disturb and offend the white girls in the class. After speaking further with Sarah, however, Prudence quickly saw how earnestly the girl wanted to learn, and she decided to let her into the school. "By this act," wrote Prudence, "I gave great offence."

Almost immediately the parents of the white students complained angrily about Sarah's admission, and some withdrew their daughters from the school, hoping that Prudence would reconsider her decision. The louder the protests, however, the bolder Prudence's resolve became. She would not agree to dismiss Sarah from her school. In much the same way that Myrtilla came to see education as a tool in the fight against slavery, Prudence resolved to teach African American girls in Connecticut to improve their situation in society.

She sought the advice of abolitionists in Boston and Providence and requested guidance from William Lloyd Garrison. By February 1833 Prudence had made a daring decision. Not only would she not remove her one black student from her school—she had decided to dismiss the remaining white students! One month later, she announced the opening of her "High School for young colored Ladies and Misses."

The response, even in this New England village, was nothing short of outrage. The townspeople protested what they were sure would be an influx of African Americans into their neighborhoods—and the resulting decrease in their house values. They refused to sell food or medicine to the boarding students who attended Prudence's school, and local churches denied the girls admittance. The school was attacked and the students harassed by angry villagers—but Prudence Crandall's resolve only stiffened.

Soon the citizens of Canterbury brought their concerns to the Connecticut state legislature, seeking a legal way to close Prudence's school. On May 24, 1833, lawmakers unanimously passed what would come to be known as the "Black Law" of Connecticut—a bill that outlawed any school from teaching black students from outside of the state. Since many of Prudence's students were from New York, Pennsylvania, and Massachusetts, her school was now against the laws of Connecticut. Still, Prudence was unmoved.

On June 27, 1833, she was arrested by a local sheriff and jailed for violating the Black Law of Connecticut. Though she was soon released on bail, she spent the next several months embroiled in a bitter and contentious legal battle that became headline news across the region. After a trial, a hung jury, a guilty verdict, an appeal, and ultimately a reversal, Prudence was cleared of wrongdoing and was legally allowed to continue her school.

Where the law failed, however, Canterbury's citizens would shamefully succeed. With the continuation and promised growth of Prudence's school, the attacks by local rowdies increased and became more violent and dangerous. On several occasions the school was ransacked by men with clubs and then partially burned. It was finally enough for Prudence. In

September 1834, fearing for the safety of her students, she closed her school for good.

For years to come, the case against Prudence Crandall symbolized the harsh racist reality faced by many in the United States—and served as a warning to those who tried to change that reality. Myrtilla Miner could never have known that one day attitudes would change and that Prudence Crandall would ultimately be viewed as a heroine for justice and equality in Canterbury and beyond.

But as Myrtilla made her way to Washington, DC, in 1851 to teach the African American daughters of the slaveholding South, she did know that she was entering a powder keg of anger and racial anxiety that threatened not only her well-intentioned plans but her personal safety as well.

7

"THE SCHOOL FOR COLORED GIRLS"

"Character is what the age calls for," Myrtilla had written in an early essay. "If you can do a good deed or a noble and true one, do it. Care not for the 'opinion of the world.'"

On December 3, 1851, Myrtilla cast off her fears and the doubts of others and opened her "School for Colored Girls," as it came to be known, with six free African American students in attendance. She no doubt began class with a brief introduction of who she was and then described what she expected from her students. Her stern yet caring approach to education would have been apparent from the moment she spoke—as well as her unwavering commitment to equality. She explained to the class that the color of their skin had nothing to do with their ability to learn—but that attitudes in the community and the country as a whole would require that they work harder and show more restraint than white schoolchildren. "Be as wise as serpents and as harmless as doves," they were taught.

Edward C. Yonnger, a black man living freely in Washington, DC, had offered Myrtilla a small room in his house on

A typical neighborhood scene in Washington, DC, in the 1850s. *Prints & Photographs Division, Library of Congress, LC-USZ62-110975*

11th Street near New York Avenue to be used as a schoolroom. Yonnger risked much in providing his home for the black children's school, but Myrtilla had no doubt conveyed in her passionate and insistent manner the importance of her mission and the uncertainty of its fate without outside assistance.

Myrtilla described herself at the time as "an entire stranger in the community to both white and colored." Nearly penniless, she was completely dependent upon the aid and kindness of others, and she constantly sought the support of donors throughout the city and beyond. She was amazed and saddened by the unwillingness of many who spoke of charity and goodwill to offer any assistance at all. Her faith in God remained strong, however, and as classes began she remained certain that "the majesty of righteousness has surrounded the school."

One of the first things Myrtilla attempted to do upon her arrival in Washington, DC, was to seek political support for her cause. She communicated her plans to the city mayor, Walter Lenox, and was encouraged to learn that he approved of her school and was willing to advise her. After he canceled several appointments with her, however, Lenox sent word that "official reasons" prevented him from meeting with her. The meeting would never take place.

Lacking support from the mayor, Myrtilla went right to the top. On several occasions she called upon the president of the United States, Millard Fillmore, at the Executive Mansion—what we now call the White House—and requested a meeting. When told on each visit that the president was busy and unable to meet with her, Myrtilla left her calling card. Having received no reply from the president, she wrote an angry letter scolding him on his manners. "Allow me to suggest," she wrote, "that it might, at least, seem more gentlemanly, when you receive the card of a lady, asking an audience to inform her, when she may call & hope to see you if you are occupied at that hour."

As Myrtilla attempted to gather political support, she also started recruiting students. It proved to be a complex task. She wavered between the need to maintain secrecy to avoid opposition and the need to publicize her project enough to gain students and support.

Her reputation as a quality teacher soon spread, and as word circulated among the African American community, the number of pupils very quickly surged. After the first month, she was teaching 15, and by the second, over 40. "How beautiful my school of 45 colored girls is . . . ," she wrote to her brother in early 1852. "Some are very dark & others are fairer & more beautiful than we. Some have red hair & blue eyes . . . & some

are exquisitely beautiful, with their fine dark curls and eyes &
slightly tinged complexions."

Myrtilla's first students ranged in age from 7 to 17. Many of
them came from the more well-to-do black families of Washington, DC, and even John Cook, the headmaster of the Smothers
School, would later request that Myrtilla accept his own daughter
as her student. To help defray the growing expenses of the school,
Myrtilla imposed an annual tuition of $15, though she often
admitted a student with no means to pay if the girl had a particular eagerness to learn. And there was no doubt of the school's mission. "The present promise is," wrote Myrtilla, "that when these
girls are mature, many of them will become teachers and by their
refinement and good morals exert such an influence upon their
associates as shall relieve the world of much degradation and consequent misery." She couldn't have known it at the time, but the
School for Colored Girls was, in fact, the first teacher training
institute for African American females in the United States.

———◆—◆———

Several of Myrtilla's students told her that they had attended
or even graduated from some of the other African American
schools around the city. She learned, however, that the quality of
those schools was well below her own high standards. Though
able to read simple words and sentences, the students had little
understanding of what they were reading. They spoke and wrote
using poor grammar, and while professing knowledge of arithmetic, they could neither read nor write numbers or complete
simple calculations. Perhaps most concerning to her, however,
was the lack of basic manners, maturity, and refinement in her
students. The education she intended to bring would go beyond
simple knowledge; Myrtilla would teach them to be ladies.

Immediately upon opening her school, she definitively rejected the commonly believed myth that African Americans could not or should not be taught. "I do unequivocally assert," she later wrote, "that I find no difference of native talent, where similar advantages are enjoyed, between Anglo-Saxons and Africo-Americans." When one local citizen, Mrs. L. F. Dewey, came to visit the school and then wrote a letter to the students suggesting that black children may be educated "to a point beyond that which will be most happy for them," a class discussion resulted and Myrtilla requested that the students express their feelings on paper.

"She gains the heart of some white people, but she does not gain the heart of God. I will try to get all the education I can, and will try to do good with it, in teaching others and making them better," wrote Sarah Shorter. Nine-year-old Lizzie Snowden recorded, "I will be learned. I must be learned! I would ask her if colored people should not enjoy every right as white people?" Mary Brent eloquently proclaimed, "Though men enslave the body they cannot enslave the mind and prevent it from thinking. When we have obtained our complete Education I hope we may use well the means God has given us . . . that we may teach the Ignorant how to read as well as we." And Emily Fisher charitably wrote, "I hope Mrs. Dewey will not think we can be angry with her for what she said."

Perhaps to Mrs. Dewey's displeasure, Myrtilla's teaching methods clearly equaled or exceeded those of white schools. She exposed her "scholars," as she endearingly referred to her students, to a wide variety of guest lectures, field trips, and practical lessons on manners and personal hygiene. On several occasions, Mary Tyler Peabody, the wife of the famed educator Horace Mann, delivered lectures on grammar, and her niece provided art and drawing instruction. The fiery abolitionist and progressive writer Rev. Moncure D. Conway gave lectures on the origin of words, and Walter W. Johnson taught lessons on astronomy and constellations. One Northern publisher contributed books on many subjects, including mathematics, philosophy, history, English grammar, zoology, and orthography. The list of subjects Myrtilla taught also included reading, composition, and French translation.

The class took trips to local attractions including to a doctor's laboratory and a fair at the United States Patent Office. On some excursions the students were turned away or quickly shuffled off because of the color of their skin. During one such trip to the Smithsonian Institute, the class was reportedly asked to leave; Myrtilla complied without incident but shrewdly exited with the children through the farthest door so they could continue viewing the exhibits.

Myrtilla also used the teaching technique of letter writing to expand the views and abilities of her students. Each week the children were required to write a letter to some prominent American citizen, and by doing so they gained the valuable lessons of writing and penmanship while at the same time getting to know a variety of distinguished people such as Frederick Douglass, Harriet Beecher Stowe, and many others.

Essays and composition were required activities in Myrtilla's classroom. The children were often asked to construct sentences and write stories to strengthen their creative expression. Matilda Jones wrote the following story in 1854, demonstrating her writing ability and strong sense of morality:

The two little Girls

There were two little girls who lived in a city, but I must not tell where they lived, nor what were their names. Sometimes they were very good, & sometimes quite naughty, one was farther advanced in her studies than the other. Persons have often thought that they were sisters. They were very affection-ate to each other, one was mother-less, but the other had both father & mother. If one had anything the other was sure to get part of it.

Their fathers sent them both to a nice school, & the teacher was very fond of them. One day as they were going home from school, one of them fell into a pond. She was very much fright-ened & was afraid she should die & she said, "I shall certainly die! Oh Lord please don't let me die! Let me go home to Aunt Becky"! She had been told by her uncle not to go there, & her distress shows that little girls should not disobey their parents.

This is a true story and the little girls are members of this school. I would like you to guess who they are.

Myrtilla encouraged her students to express their opinions on a variety of topics. The children often wrote about religion and the human condition. Of course, the suffering of enslaved people was a common theme at the school.

———•◆•———

The unending need for funding and supplies required that Myr-tilla continually seek the support of others to keep her school open and thriving. When not teaching her scholars, she con-stantly requested the aid of publishers and philanthropists with the goal of securing books, supplies, and money for the school. "I rise early and toil late to accomplish well my work," she wrote to a friend in Smethport, Pennsylvania. "You should see all the let-ters I write . . . and see all the people I am obliged to call upon . . . and see the many times I walk a mile to accomplish this, besides teaching five days in the week and doing most of my sewing."

Soon the pressures and stress of the work would begin to take its toll. "I am already very thin and pale," she noted in a letter.

The outreach for support, grueling as it often was, took many forms. Within days of her arrival in Washington, Myrtilla made a point of observing the open debates in the halls of Congress. She identified her old friend Senator William Seward and soon wrote to him seeking suggestions and assistance for her newly opened school. "I should be delighted to have you look in upon us to see if we are worthy the aid of philanthropists," she wrote.

Among Myrtilla's strongest supporters was a group of Philadelphia Quakers called the Society of Friends, who were dedicated to women's rights and the abolition of slavery. Samuel Rhoads, an active leader of the society and publisher of its literary journal, *Friends' Review*, began corresponding with Mrytilla very early on and took a keen interest in her work. With the help of other like-minded Northerners, he provided money and detailed guidance for the school. Together with Harriet Beecher Stowe, the world-famous author of *Uncle Tom's Cabin*, Samuel would prove to be an unfailing ally to Myrtilla, working tirelessly to generate aid and funding from good-hearted sponsors.

Soon other wealthy Philadelphians associated with Samuel, such as Thomas Williamson, George W. Taylor, and Jasper Cope, as well as charitable and religious organizations in New York and other Northern states also became Myrtilla's supporters. From these "Friends," she received much of the financial and emotional backing to develop her school and to keep it going. "All must have failed for want of means & credit . . . ," she wrote to Harriet Beecher Stowe, "had not the Friends of Philadelphia kindly accepted by faith what no one had yet seen, the promise of the future."

In later writings and public appeals, Myrtilla left the impression that she was alone when she began her school. To be sure, the idea and preparations were hers, but the Philadelphia Quakers who supported her cause also sent a Rhode Island schoolteacher named Anna Inman to assist in the school's opening.

~~~~~~

The Society of Friends

The Religious Society of Friends, now commonly referred to as the Quakers, is a Christian religion founded in England by George Fox in the mid-1600s. As a young man, Fox became disillusioned with the teachings of conventional religions and, acting upon what he believed was a revelation from God, spent the rest of his life preaching the idea of Inward Light or Inner Light—the concept that the spirit of God is within every human being. The religious following that developed focused on silent devotional worship, simple lifestyles, and clean living. The Quakers considered themselves to be friends of Jesus and would ultimately come to be known simply as "Friends." Upon migration to the United States in the 1600s, the Friends were met with anger and persecution, but over time they were able to establish thriving communities in Rhode Island, West Jersey, and Pennsylvania. The Society of Friends became very well known for their care and concern for the poor and for their strong support of the abolitionist movement. In the early to mid-19th century a number of organizations sponsored by the Quakers were formed to carry out social reforms, including the opposition to slavery. These groups provided the workforce and financial backing for many of the progressive movements of the day.

~~~~~~

Anna's involvement was short-lived, however; though she worked with Myrtilla in the early days of the school and helped with initial arrangements, she did not play a significant role in the school's formation. A personality conflict between the two women led to Anna's early departure.

Through Myrtilla's hard work and faithful dedication, word of the school began to spread among people who shared her vision for racial justice. She began receiving donations from US congressmen, educators, and abolitionists. Harriett Beecher Stowe and her brother Henry Ward Beecher helped to discreetly publicize the details of Myrtilla's good work throughout New England and beyond, and encouraged those who could to contribute money. Even Laban Olby and his wife, the sole African Americans in Myrtilla's hometown of North Brookfield, New York, sent a small donation to the school.

———•◆•———

Along with initial success came the predictable dangers. Myrtilla wanted to take black education in Washington, DC, a step beyond what it had ever been before. Her goal was not only that African American girls would be taught but also that those girls would themselves become teachers in the black community. She knew that the slaveholding South would be studying her with wary and scornful eyes. As Ellen O'Connor later wrote, "The malignant and jealous spirit of slavery which watched over the national capital was not disposed to tolerate that anything but the merest rudiments of learning should be dispensed to the free people of color, [who were] so closely allied to the slaves in blood and sympathy."

Almost immediately upon the establishment of the School for Colored Girls, local hostilities began. Within the first several months of the school's existence, intimidation and threats of violence to Myrtilla's landlords compelled her to move its location two separate times, ultimately forcing it "nearly out of town." She personally endured insults and contempt from local residents and had difficulty finding a place to live, "because I would teach colored girls." Samuel Rhoads implored Myrtilla to carry on her work in the city as quietly as she could without stirring anger. When she told him of the threats she had received, he wrote, "Thou will not of course, give [the school] up unless compelled to do so by 'force of arms.'"

One evening in March 1852, Myrtilla had a confrontation with a disgruntled neighbor to the school that demonstrated in unsettling clarity the anger and intolerance she was up against. The neighbor, a local lawyer, encountered a small group of Myrtilla's students making their way home from the school, then located on F Street, between 18th and 19th Streets. As the girls passed by along the sidewalk, the lawyer purposefully extended his elbows in an effort to nudge them off the walkway. He swore at the girls and angrily accused them of getting in his way. He then stormed off to the African American woman who rented the classroom space to Myrtilla and demanded that she "turn out that nigger school or be mobbed." He complained that the "impertinent hussies" who attended the school were driving white people from the sidewalks and that if something wasn't immediately done the landlord could expect to see her building "torn down over her head."

Terrified, the landlord approached Myrtilla and explained what had happened, cautioning that the house was her only place to live and that she could not risk a mob. The two spoke for a while and soon Myrtilla calmed the woman down and persuaded her to trust God to protect her.

Soon, however, another man sent by the same lawyer called on the landlord and offered to find another tenant to pay the same amount that Myrtilla paid for the classroom, if she would simply evict the school. Again, greatly upset, she visited Myrtilla and explained her predicament. Myrtilla promised to seek help from the mayor. The next day she walked through the snow to the office of the new mayor, John Maury, only to be frustrated that he was "too much a politician" to get involved.

Realizing that a direct confrontation with the lawyer was now inevitable, the next day Myrtilla dressed as finely as her wardrobe would allow, "knowing the importance a Southerner attaches to the outer man," and went directly to the lawyer's office.

"After introducing myself and being received with great politeness I said that I came to inquire respecting my pupils, that I understood they disturbed him in returning home from school two evenings since."

"Your pupils?" inquired the lawyer.

"Yes, the colored girls."

"What you keep that nigger school?" asked the lawyer.

Myrtilla confirmed that, yes, the school was hers and that she visited the lawyer to learn of the details surrounding his complaint. "I hold myself responsible for their deportment in the street and I have called to learn the head and front of their offending."

"Well," he said, "I'll tell you, we are not going to have this nigger school, anyhow . . . for they are saucy and impudent and shove white people off the walks! It is contrary to all rules to have them gathered in such companies and we sha'nt have it!"

Doubting the trustworthiness of the man's story, Myrtilla asked, "Did more than one answer you?"

"Yes, they all answered as saucy as possible."

"That tells too much," replied Myrtilla, "for I have forbidden my pupils to ever answer the *insults* of white men. What did you say to my scholars?"

Now the tables were turned and the lawyer became defensive. Ignoring the question, he responded with his true complaint. "We are not going to have you Northern Abolitionists coming down here to teach our niggers. We know better what to do with them than you do."

"What do you propose to do with them?" asked Myrtilla.

"Send them out of the country," he said. "We don't want them here. . . . I have an idea that they have grown more impertinent since you came among them. . . . Who sent you here to teach niggers?"

She stiffened, then proudly said, "A higher power than man directed me and <u>man</u> shall not defeat me."

"Well you will be mobbed; that will be the consequence," came the angry retort.

Myrtilla questioned the "Southern chivalry" of any man who would attack a defenseless woman or cause others to do so and added, "It would be well to remember that we are on national domain and the laws are for me as well as for you."

The lawyer bristled and angrily stamped his foot out of frustration. "No!" he shouted. "This is every inch my own soil. Every inch mine on which we stand!"

Sensing that she had won the point, she continued, "But you can make no law, for they are made by the legislators of the country for my protection and for my scholars as well as for you. Besides," she added, "these free colored people are not your niggers and you have no more right to say what I shall or shall not do with them than I have to say what you shall do. Inasmuch as I do not presume to dictate to you, neither shall you interfere with me or my plans."

Flustered by the truth of Myrtilla's argument, the lawyer now changed tactics. He asked, "But what good will it do to teach them? They will never thank you. They are a most ungrateful set and will only turn and despise you for all you do."

"I should so suppose from the treatment they have received," said Myrtilla. "But I am not seeking thanks and these considerations are of little consequence compared with the law of right."

Again, the lawyer threatened her with a mob and the destruction of her school, insisting that local newspapers would carry the story of the "white abolitionist that came down here to teach a nigger school" and was mobbed.

She quickly responded that the news articles from the next day would identify this lawyer as the one who instigated the mob. "And then we shall no longer remain in obscurity but stand side by side before the world for judgment and I shall be more willing to take my sentence than you."

"It was a strong conflict of words, fast and ready, lasting more than an hour," Myrtilla later recalled. "I assured him that I might rest in peace and that I was resolved to teach this school at the hazard of my life, if need be; that I feared no man."

Though she had clearly won the moral argument with the disgruntled lawyer, she remained at that location for only another month and then secured other space in order to protect and calm the woman who owned the property. "The mob died in embryo and the school awakened to newness of life."

The hostilities and threats continued, however, at Myrtilla's next location on K Street near the Western Market. "When opposition and persecution came as they did come with much power," she wrote, ". . . wisdom allowed me to ward off those evils which threatened to reduce my fair school . . . to a ruin." Myrtilla responded to threats of mobs and fires and whippings with faith in God and unshakable courage. "If it is [God's] work, and he has permitted me to be the instrument of its commencement, no man or men can frustrate the design, and all their efforts will prove unavailing."

Myrtilla's scholars, burdened and oppressed as they may have been, greatly appreciated their teacher. The many letters of gratitude written by her students heartened Myrtilla and no doubt demonstrated that the unthinkable risks she had undertaken were worth it all.

"Miss Miner you will remember that I could not write anything fit to be read one year ago, for I could neither write intelligently nor think anything sensible enough to pay for the trouble of writing . . . ," wrote Mary Shorter. "I am not able being a child to express my thanks for the pains you have taken with me in endeavoring to teach me not merely book-knowledge but to be moral and lady-like, that I may be useful to society."

Another student praised Myrtilla for teaching morals and the commandments of God. She added in her letter, "I think our Teacher is very kind to teach us to be entelegent [sic] and punschul [sic] in our duty." The young student signed the letter, "Your dutiful Scholar."

And Lizzie Snowden, in a letter to friends, praised her school and the knowledge she received there. "I love my teacher very much," she wrote.

Myrtilla expected much from her scholars. Her meticulous attention to detail, moral standing, and cultural awareness became well known to the students themselves as well as their families. But her expectations surged far beyond normal classroom studies and etiquette. To Myrtilla Miner, the School for Colored Girls was her way to strike a blow against the institution of slavery itself.

"On you more than on any other depends the emancipation of 4,000,000 . . . people in this country," her students were told.

GROWING PAINS

Myrtilla was tremendously proud of her school. Against all odds she had traveled to an unfamiliar city and quietly gone about the work of educating young girls of color despite angry and determined opposition. In October 1852 she wrote to a friend, "I love this school of mine profoundly."

Public curiosity in Myrtilla and her work grew, and visitors to the school became a regular occurrence. In the first four months of 1853 alone, Myrtilla hosted over 100 guests. A visitor, Rev. Orville Dewey, wrote, "It is really an attractive spectacle—bright faces—and appearance of as much intelligence as I see in any other Schools—as quick and ready answers to questions—as much neatness, order and good behavior."

One morning an educator from Philadelphia, Margaret Robinson, arrived at the school only to be informed by a student that Myrtilla was away on school business. Disappointed by the news and expecting unsupervised chaos among the students, Margaret was astonished to find complete order in the classroom. She was politely invited in by one of the students and watched with pleasure as each child occupied herself with schoolwork. Thereafter the older, more advanced students led the class in a reading exercise followed by arithmetic tables, all without fuss or confusion. In a short while Myrtilla arrived, bid her visitor hello, and resumed the classwork as if she had been there from the start.

Soon letters began to come from locations as far away as Great Britain expressing words of encouragement and praise. From the western part of the United States, one letter-writer applauded:

> The educational movement of those noble young women among the colored inhabitants of Washington city was altogether new to me and somewhat surprising. I did not expect that such an effort would be *tolerated* by the authorities of that city—much less countenanced. The result is truly cheering and an evidence of some progress.

The ever-steady and cautious Samuel Rhoads, however, reminded Myrtilla that the encouragement of others, though welcome, may not always be relied upon when difficult times approach.

As word of Myrtilla's school circulated through the black neighborhoods and churches of Washington, DC, demand steadily rose for her services. Mothers and fathers pleaded for her to educate their daughters, but lack of space and funding often forced her to refuse—though ultimately she sometimes relented and agreed to take them in. Local hostilities were not the only reason why Myrtilla continually moved the location of her school in the early months of its existence; she needed more space for an ever-growing number of students. Renting small rooms from brave and charitable citizens would no longer be sufficient. It became overwhelmingly clear that she needed to secure a larger and more permanent location for the school.

The Philadelphia Quakers, Samuel Rhoads, Thomas Williamson, and Jasper Cope, who were actively involved in the school's aid and growth, enthusiastically supported the idea, and they soon began a fundraising campaign to purchase a lot upon which to build a permanent school.

Though she was receiving much encouragement and money from her Northern friends, Myrtilla was solely responsible for the daily operation and maintenance of the school. Being virtually isolated in Washington, DC, she alone taught lessons, interviewed new students, dealt with local finances, secured supplies, fended off hostilities, and made political friends. By the first summer of the school's existence, she was exhausted and felt sick, but the quest to find a new location for the school and to raise money for its purchase kept her moving and motivated.

Throughout much of that summer, after the semester ended, she traveled north in a tireless mission to raise money. She met with wealthy donors and spoke to abolitionist groups about the work she was doing in the nation's capital. Through these efforts she secured loans of about $2,500 and gifts totaling $610, and she strengthened relationships with the Philadelphia Friends as well as with the Beecher family in New England. Thomas Williamson agreed to become the school's accountant, and he used his financial skills to properly invest the money while plans for the new location were finalized.

By the early months of 1853, after a few setbacks, a permanent site for the School for Colored Girls was agreed upon. Located between 19th and 20th Streets, N and O Streets, and New Hampshire Avenue in Washington, DC, the property included "a small frame house and barn, and many fruit and shade trees." "It is a whole square of ground, comprising more than three acres, a little out of town, a thriving neighborhood, convenient to the market, etc.," wrote Myrtilla excitedly. Finding the location was one thing, but finalizing the deal proved to be quite another. Her school was growing, she had an expanding group of supporters, and her scholars were receiving an education beyond anything previously available to them. Though it seemed that everything was finally coming together for Myrtilla, trouble was brewing ahead.

In a letter to a friend, Myrtilla described March 4, 1853, her 38th birthday—and Inauguration Day for the new president, Franklin Pierce—as "noisy, boisterous, stormy, and fatiguing, just as I *never* wish a birthday to be.

It was, perhaps, a premonition of things to come.

———— •·• ————

Myrtilla described her own personality as being marked by "indiscretions and eccentricities." Her brash tendencies often turned people off and sometimes caused problems. She expected perfection from herself and others and often proved difficult to work with. At least one person who initially agreed to help her in Washington, DC, thought better of it after witnessing her pushiness, and he thereafter did his best to avoid her. As one historian wrote, "Her perfectionism and self-righteousness, combined with a restless drive approaching anxiety, kept her constantly keyed up. To her admirers she was strong, determined, and energetic, but to those with whom she crossed swords—and their number grew—she was willful, unreasonable, and impetuous."

The difficult work of finalizing a permanent location for the school revealed flaws in Myrtilla's character and strained her relationships like never before. Though the new school site had been chosen and the owner was willing to sell, legal problems plagued the process and slowed things down to a standstill. The title to the property had not been properly cleared, and the existing occupants refused to leave.

Either not fully understanding the issues with the property or simply not caring, Myrtilla saw no reason why she couldn't immediately just move her school in even though the title had not yet changed hands. As she had very little money of her own, it would have been almost impossible for her to purchase the land herself; thus Samuel and Thomas formed an informal trust to take ownership when the legal issues were ultimately resolved. They, in essence, would handle all the financial matters of the transaction and would make final decisions as to the property for the benefit of Myrtilla and her students.

Without full control, however, Myrtilla became suspicious of her Quaker friends and irrationally accused them of sabotaging the project. Samuel and Thomas were rightfully prudent with all donated money and refused to release any funds for the land purchase until the legal problems were resolved. In her impatience, Myrtilla made wild claims against the two men of obstruction and neglect in finalizing the deal. To Myrtilla, she and her students were being victimized by remote businessmen who did not understand the depths of the problems faced in Washington, DC. There was simply no excuse for the delays, she believed.

During this stressful period, Myrtilla's behavior turned rather peculiar and unbalanced. She was terribly unhappy and seemed to take out her anger on others. She wrote heated letters to her Philadelphia supporters, complaining of her difficulties and impulsively blaming her problems on others. She felt that the world was against her, and at times she would lose control of her emotions. On one afternoon the parent of a student even noticed with alarm that his daughter had returned home from school severely beaten and bruised from a thrashing with a stick. Myrtilla, it seemed, had reacted cruelly to behavior that she found unacceptable. One moment she could be joyfully instructing her class—and the next flying off the handle in a violent rage. "She was often severe in her kindness, as no doubt, many of her old pupils will remember," wrote one friend. "Perfectly intolerant of bad odors . . . [and] untidiness . . . it must be said of her . . . that she was not always patient of spirit. . . . Her whole living was intense."

Adding to Myrtilla's problems was a terrible sense of vulnerability and loneliness. She saw herself as one against the world—a solitary warrior for justice. She was so single minded and focused on her work that the idea of marriage seemed preposterous, and yet she yearned for the closeness of romantic love. Her absolute dedication to her school, though satisfying in a professional and moral sense, had left a void in her heart.

Perhaps from this void came her odd obsession with a young man named Walpole Cecil.

About 20 years younger than Myrtilla, Walpole was a biracial man who had run away from enslavement and who simultaneously showed both great promise and certain failure. His past and background were a complete mystery. Perhaps that was what attracted her to him. They met in early 1853 while boarding in the same Washington, DC, rooming house.

Perhaps aided by his good looks and adolescent charm, Walpole had been offered several opportunities for employment, but on each occasion he let people down and turned to crime. To the grave concern of Myrtilla's friends and Northern benefactors, she took a strange and even fanatic liking to the boy and began dedicating much of her time and energy to his care and protection. She begged him to change his ways and insisted that he study the Bible and turn his life to God. To Myrtilla, Walpole was a well-intentioned and misunderstood victim of society. To the rest of the world, he was a conniving scoundrel.

In an effort to avoid arrest for his petty crimes, Walpole fled to Baltimore, and for several days, Myrtilla followed him, devoting herself to his well-being and pleading for him to change his behavior. For months they exchanged countless letters, and she met with him on many occasions to counsel and advise him.

Myrtilla's interest in Walpole soon morphed into an obsession; she even began researching his history with the purpose of writing a book about his life—and she wrote several chapters. She fought to keep him out of jail and pleaded with her Philadelphia friends to help him. Samuel flatly refused to have any contact with the boy and warned Myrtilla that her school could be in jeopardy because of the time she spent on Walpole. Others warned her that Walpole had deceived her with his handsome face and alluring charisma. The relationship, wrote one observer, "became a standing joke" among those who knew her.

Myrtilla was undeterred. She sent Walpole to a friend in Boston for employment who quickly found him to be untrustworthy and undeserving of Myrtilla's efforts. She scolded him, but her letters revealed the depth of her feelings toward him: "In spite of all your faults I love you most tenderly."

Myrtilla finally advised Walpole to either find work on a ship or travel to Africa to avoid jail in the United States. It is possible that he followed her instructions, for in the fall of 1853 their correspondence ended. Earlier in the year Myrtilla had expressed her tender feelings for Walpole in a letter to a friend:

How I wish I could take his hand & look into his eyes once more, for my soul has labored for his soul with a yearning which nothing but a God-power could awaken in one of stern spirit like me—& this letter goes to you with the treasure of my *tears* upon it—A harvest that has not been gathered till *now*.

In October 1853, while others continued to work out the legal issues with the new property, Myrtilla reopened her school in two rented rooms in Washington, DC. It would be her fourth location and the start of her third year.

The school was steadily growing, and Myrtilla was able to take on an assistant by charging $1.50 per month to any of the students who could afford the payment. It seemed that Myrtilla was able to put aside her feelings for Walpole and once again focus on her work. "When the school did open this month, the pupils rushed in so happy in the appreciation of the blessing, so healthy in study, so neat in appearance, and so quiet in manners, that I have experienced only joy in teaching them," she wrote. Threats and hostilities from local agitators continued, of course, but when the students assembled in wonderful calm and order, the anger seemed to subside. "Why, I never see nicer looking scholars in my life; nobody will disturb these!" said the man who rented the rooms to Myrtilla.

At about this time she received a generous gift for her school from Harriet Beecher Stowe. Harriet's book *Uncle Tom's Cabin* was by now an international success and earning sizable royalties. From the profits, Harriet sent Myrtilla $1,000, which she received "with a heart filled of gratitude [and] thankfulness." The gift helped pay the extensive costs of the land purchase and the ongoing expenses of running the school, and Harriet had given it with great confidence in its recipient. "She has been gifted by nature with singular talents for this work," she wrote of Myrtilla, "and endowed by God's grace with a courage, zeal, and devotion such as are given to but a few."

In March 1854, the legal problems with the new property were at long last resolved, and the permanent location for Myrtilla's School for Colored Girls was finalized. The lot and its buildings cost $4,300, of which $2,000 had been previously contributed and about $2,300 borrowed. The work, however, was only beginning. The long-fought-for property was, according to Myrtilla, "in a most forlorn and desolate condition, with no fence to bound its broad acres . . . , no security to its old clattering houses, locks and bolts, blinds and fastenings, seeming to have had a general rebellion and 'stepped out.'"

Along with her generous gift, Harriet also made arrangements for Emily Edmonson to come to Washington, DC, to assist at the school. Emily had formerly been enslaved, and Henry Ward Beecher had helped purchase her freedom. She had become an antislavery ambassador of sorts and was well known throughout the abolitionist community. Myrtilla, pleased to have Emily's support since her current assistant was in ill health, quickly concluded that Emily had natural teaching ability and would surely become qualified as a take-charge instructor. Emily's parents and several of her siblings rented one of the buildings on the property to help meet the costs of upkeep.

As word of the larger and now permanent location for an African American school started to spread, local hostilities once again began to fester. Shortly after moving into the new property Myrtilla received an ominous note signed by the "Citizens of the First Ward," threatening, "If you are not out of that house with your niggers by the tenth of April you and all your effects

The Edmonson Sisters

Mary and Emily Edmonson were born in Maryland, the daughters of a free African American man and an enslaved woman. The law declared that the sisters were automatically enslaved at birth because of their mother's legal status. On April 16, 1848, the Edmonson sisters and 75 other enslaved people became part of a daring escape attempt. In a plan hatched by the antislavery activist William Chaplin and likely financed by Gerrit Smith, Mary, Emily, and the others quietly boarded the schooner *Pearl*, docked at a Washington, DC, wharf. At about midnight the ship, carrying the huddled stowaways, left the dock and made its way down the Potomac River. The *Pearl* was soon captured and returned to Washington, however, where an angry crowd had gathered to meet it. Along with the others, Mary and Emily were immediately returned to slavery while their father tried desperately to stop their planned sale to the New Orleans slave market, where they would surely be mistreated. The sad plight of the Edmonson sisters quickly spread throughout the North, and soon Rev. Henry Ward Beecher led an effort to buy their freedom. Rescued from a life of slavery and transported to New York, Mary and Emily learned to read and write. They became instant celebrities in the North and were regularly invited to speak at antislavery rallies, where they shared tales of their harrowing experiences. In the years that followed, the sisters attended Oberlin College in Ohio, and their story was immortalized by Harriet Beecher Stowe in a chapter of *Uncle Tom's Cabin*.

will be set in flames." Having worked far too hard to yield to threats of violence Myrtilla and Emily refused to give in—but the aggression continued. On a regular basis neighborhood hooligans threw rocks at the house and shouted angry threats at Myrtilla and her students. "Emily and I lived here alone, unprotected, except by God," wrote Myrtilla to a friend, "the rowdies occasionally stoning our house at evening, and we nightly retiring in the expectation that the house would be fired by morning." Once, when the attacks were particularly violent, Myrtilla rushed out of the building and ran a square block shouting for help. Within 15 minutes four "very savage-looking men" armed with clubs appeared in front of the house and pledged to keep a watchful eye.

Despite the occasional assistance of neighbors and her strong faith in God's protection, Myrtilla soon erected a "hard-to-get-over picket fence" and also made a public showing of pistol practice to discourage local rowdies who threatened her school and harassed her students. When one evening a crowd had congregated outside, throwing stones and hurling insults, she made her way to the window and, waving her revolver, informed the horde in no uncertain terms that she would shoot the first man to come to the door. "Mob my school! You dare not!" she shouted. "If you tear it down over my head I shall get another house. There is no law to prevent my teaching these people, and I shall teach them, even unto death!"

One of her pupils later wrote, "She was one of the bravest women I have ever known."

EXHILARATION
AND EXHAUSTION

In 1854 the uneasy standoff between North and South was once again tested. Since the Missouri Compromise of 1820, the thorny legal question of slavery in the United States had been skillfully calmed and violent conflict between the states had been avoided. Beyond certain declared boundaries, the institution of slavery was not permitted under the compromise. When American pioneers began settling the lands of Kansas and Nebraska in the mid-1850s, however, the issue was once again thrust to the forefront.

In the halls of Congress a fierce and contentious battle took place to determine whether slavery would be allowed in these new territories. The resulting Kansas-Nebraska Act, which was narrowly passed by Congress and signed into law by President Pierce in May 1854, declared that popular sovereignty in each of the new territories would determine the question of slavery. In other words, the people of each territory would decide and vote on the issue.

~~~~~~

Missouri Compromise

In the early part of the 19th century a delicate balance between slave and free states existed in Congress and in the country as a whole. The nation had 22 states at the time, evenly divided between those allowing slavery and those prohibiting it. When Missouri requested admission to the Union as a slaveholding state in 1819, however, tensions began to grow and a heated nationwide debate took place that threatened to tear the country apart. The result in Congress was the passage of the Missouri Compromise. Under this law Missouri was admitted into the Union as a slave state, but Maine—then a territory of Massachusetts—was admitted as a free state. In an effort to diffuse tensions and settle the issue, legislators further agreed that slavery from that point forward would be prohibited in the Louisiana Territory north of an agreed-upon imaginary line. The Missouri Compromise held for 34 years and at least delayed the violent split of the country over slavery.

~~~~~~

In a cynical effort to sway the vote in Kansas and Nebraska, abolitionists from the North and proslavery agitators from the South poured into the territories, creating a powder keg of anger that often erupted into violence. The confrontation would come to be known as "Bleeding Kansas."

In Washington, DC, the School for Colored Girls continued to grow despite the anger and controversy that it sometimes generated. The ongoing debates over slavery and the congressional actions to deal with it were frequent topics for discussion

Bleeding Kansas

Coined by Horace Greeley, founder and editor of the *New-York Tribune*, the term "Bleeding Kansas" came from a violent episode beginning in 1854 surrounding the question of slavery in the Kansas Territory. The concept of popular sovereignty—the vote of the people—was used to determine the issue as required by the Kansas-Nebraska Act, in the hope that fairness and democracy would finally settle the matter. Instead, in an effort to sway the vote, thousands of proslavery activists from Missouri and antislavery abolitionists from the North poured into and settled the territory. These people were not originally from Kansas and did not really live there; they only came to ensure that their side would win on the votes concerning slavery. Separate elections were held by makeshift governments created by each side, and rampant fraud tainted the results. Anger and mistrust between the two factions ruled the day, and armed bands from both sides soon clashed in violence and bloodshed. Property was destroyed and many people were killed. The matter was finally settled in 1861 when Kansas was admitted to the Union as a free state, but Bleeding Kansas, the limited civil war that erupted over slavery, was an ominous sign of things to come.

in the classroom. Myrtilla encouraged her students to talk about the political events of the day, and they were always reminded—though they needed no reminder—of the injustice of racial inequality. When asked to compose an essay on the sad plight of American slaves, Myrtilla's student Marietta Hill wrote reflectively,

> Sometimes I think that slavery will never be abolished & then I really despair of freedoms swaying its banner over a suffering world. Sometimes a dark cloud seems to overshadow me, and since the Nebraska bill has passed the cloud appears thicker & darker—& I say will slavery forever exist? But a voice says, "It shall cease! It shall and must be abolished"! I think there will be blood shed before all can be free, and the question is, are we willing to give up our lives for freedom? Will we die for our people!

Marietta's poignant essay was both a passionate plea for justice and a gloomy premonition of war. She was not alone in her beliefs. Free and enslaved African Americans and fair-minded white citizens across the country were now coming to the realization that the Kansas-Nebraska Act was drawing the nation ever closer to civil war.

———•———

Every day, it seemed, more and more students requested admission to Myrtilla's school, and the list of inquisitive visitors continued to grow. Myrtilla's old friend and pen pal William Seward and his entire family visited often, as did other congressmen—both pro- and antislavery—virtually all agreeing on the goodness of Myrtilla's mission. Clergymen from the Washington,

DC, area and beyond were frequent visitors and reliable contributors to her cause. And Abigail Kent Means—the aunt of the First Lady of the United States—also visited on many occasions as an envoy of the president. The School for Colored Girls gained much credibility, and hostilities seemed to dissolve when local residents spotted the official presidential carriage often parked in front of Myrtilla's schoolhouse. As Ellen O'Connor wrote, "Her school became one of the places in the Capital to be seen, and visitors from all parts of the Union were almost daily to be found there."

As Myrtilla and her Northern supporters began to feel more secure in the success and resilience of the school it became apparent that the hazardous process of open, public fundraising must begin. Though money was a constant requirement for maintenance and growth, Myrtilla and her Philadelphia friends were always worried about drawing *too* much attention, so as not to arouse local or even national backlash.

Beginning in 1854 Myrtilla, Samuel Rhoads, and Thomas Williamson published an annual circular for distribution to supporters and possible donors in an effort to raise funds. It was a compromise between keeping totally quiet on the one hand, and dangerously advertising in Washington, DC, newspapers and magazines on the other. "We are now prepared to speak with a confidence that must be acceptable to all," the first address proclaimed. Of the many testimonials of Myrtilla and her school in the circular, the first was conspicuously from Dr. David Phares, Myrtilla's old friend and former employer from Mississippi. "She has manifested as a teacher . . . ," wrote Phares, "the highest moral character and unusual skill in imparting knowledge, arousing thought and [discipline] in the most rational manner, while her character at all times has been most exceptional."

One of Myrtilla's chief goals was to construct a new school-house as soon as possible. The two existing buildings at the new location were falling apart, and it was always her intention to tear them down and replace them. Indeed, the 1854 fundraising circular made reference to the construction of a "suitable building for the accommodation of the School" and stated a fundraising goal for that purpose. Though constantly restrained by her financially cautious Northern friends, Myrtilla thought big. She had always intended that her school would ultimately be large enough for 100 to 150 students, and she hoped to model it after Oberlin College near Cleveland, Ohio, the first institution to grant bachelor's degrees to women of all races.

The growth of her school and the construction of a new building were now the driving forces of Myrtilla's life. She hired an architect to draw detailed plans and specifications for a new two-story schoolhouse covering such essentials as room dimensions, window openings, doorways, masonry, roofing, and building materials. Myrtilla knew what she wanted down to the minutest detail; the question was how to achieve it.

She traveled north during her summer break of 1854 with the goal of raising money to cover building costs. As strained as her relationship with Samuel and Thomas had become during the purchase of the new school property, the Philadelphians and antislavery Friends welcomed her with excitement and admiration for the work she was doing in Washington, DC. To provide her supporters with concrete evidence of her mission, Myrtilla brought two of her best-behaved scholars with her. "How scrupulously neat she obliged them to be, and how sensitive she was on their account, as much so, it seemed to me, as if they had been her own children," wrote Emily Edmonson.

While journeying through the familiar towns of New York State in her northern fundraising effort, Myrtilla made a point

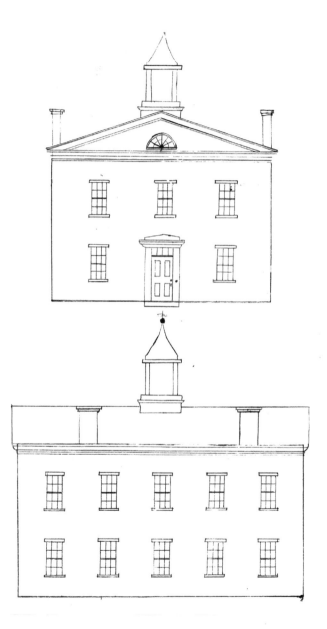

Myrtilla's plans for a new schoolhouse. *Subject file. n.d. MS Myrtilla Miner Papers: Library of Congress, Nineteenth Century Collections Online*

Oberlin College

Oberlin College, located in northern Ohio, was founded by a Presbyterian minister and a missionary in 1833. The school's purpose was to provide an educational alternative based on Christian principles to the settlers of the region. The town of Oberlin and the college that bears its name were both established with the financial assistance of several wealthy donors. From the beginning, the school was open to both men and women and, through the influence of its first president, quickly adopted and championed many progressive causes such as women's rights and abolitionism. Within two years of its opening, Oberlin began admitting African American students and was the only college to do so during that time. Deeply committed to its reformist values, Oberlin was an important stop on the Underground Railroad, providing care and assistance to people fleeing north from slavery. In the late 1800s collegiate sports found a home at Oberlin. John William Heisman was the college's first football coach in 1892, and later became the inspiration for the Heisman Trophy, an annual award given to the country's best college football player.

of visiting Frederick Douglass once again at his Rochester print shop. Unlike their first meeting three years earlier he greeted her with open arms and praised what she had accomplished in Washington, DC—though she had taken up the cause against his best advice. In what was now called *Frederick Douglass' Paper*, he publicly applauded Myrtilla after their visit and congratulated her courage and success. "Here is something being done," Frederick proudly told his readers,

> for the real elevation and advancement of the colored people of this country. A school is established at the Capitol of this republic, where the . . . daughters of the proscribed race may enjoy the privilege of attending school, and of being instructed by a competent teacher. . . . It is a thing calling for loud gratitude.

Myrtilla must have smiled to herself with satisfaction.

Despite her valiant efforts, however, her fundraising campaign fell short. Many worthy charities competed for money from churches and wealthy donors, and education was often not seen as a priority. To make matters worse, a backlash occurred when Frederick casually noted in his newspaper that the two little scholars accompanying Myrtilla on her trip were "so nearly white as to make it almost impossible for the unpracticed eye to identify them with the African race." A prominent African American businessman named George Thomas Downing objected and publicly accused Myrtilla of favoring the light-skinned students of her school. In so doing, he questioned her worthiness for support. The matter got so out of hand that Samuel Rhoads wrote a scathing rebuttal in Frederick's newspaper and included a list of tributes and references from well-known abolitionists, and a restatement of Myrtilla's antislavery credentials—in case they were doubted by supporters.

With a less-than-successful money-raising effort and racial fires to put out as a result of Frederick's article, Myrtilla returned to Washington worn out and disheartened. Moreover, Emily Edmonson, on whom she depended for assistance, was preparing to leave on a fundraising trip of her own to buy her brother's freedom from slavery. Myrtilla would be left to maintain the dilapidated houses, take care of three black children who now boarded at the property, and instruct all her students alone and without help. Lacking enough money to grow her school and faced with a large tax bill from the city that had arrived while she was gone, Myrtilla's outlook began to falter. She soon showed signs of weakness and disillusionment, and at times her confidence in herself and others collapsed.

Despite her public pronouncements of praise and hope for her students, privately Myrtilla was losing patience with them. "My strength & faith almost fail at times but I am still pressed into service, & toil on like one doomed to do his task & die," she wrote. And intolerance—even racism—seemed to get the best of her:

> This work was for me to perform, unquestionably . . . but tho' there are many lights & beauties in it . . . there are disagreeables that try my soul to the very foundation . . . such are the slackiness, stupidity, laziness & filthiness of the majority of these people . . . & were I not a christian I know I should relinquish the effort & let the next generation follow the last in all their stupidity and folly.

Her students' parents began to notice a change in Myrtilla's personality. Her obsessive focus on cleanliness and her blind insistence that every harsh and rigid school rule, no matter how trivial, be followed caused the parents much worry and concern. One day, after Myrtilla severely punished her student

Mary Brent for some trivial offense, the girl's parents nervously approached Myrtilla and asked whether she needed to adhere so strictly to her code of conduct.

The result was predictable wrath. Myrtilla lashed out, scolding the parents for daring to question her authority and threatening to remove their daughter from the school if she could not follow her rules. In a long and overdramatic letter to the girl's family Myrtilla wrote, "If you continue to conflict with the good of the school in this manner, it will prove to you only a curse. . . . May your eyes be opened to comprehend what dreadful endurance is involved in this mission to raise a people who constantly turn back to their idols. . . ." She then signed off, "Farewell (I only pray God to let me die) . . . ," adding the bitter postscript, "Enemies of colored people will exalt over yours if you repent not. Slaveholders will tell me, 'I told you so!'"

By the start of 1855 Myrtilla was totally exhausted, and her health was once again failing. She suffered from bouts of depression and endured constant severe headaches that left her with what she later described as a "partial derangement of the brain." She was often unable to teach, and for days at a time the students conducted classes without her. She would later confess how low she had sunk. "I was a pitiable invalid," she wrote to a friend, "still trying to teach, or at least, keeping up my school, while really approaching that stage of nervous sensitiveness and irritability which ends in insanity."

Her aggressive behavior was not limited to attacks on others. At her lowest points she would even masochistically harm herself. "Her hands, without any will of her own, would beat the diseased parts of her body severely . . . daily for five hours," wrote one acquaintance in whom Myrtilla had confided.

Consumed by suicidal thoughts, Myrtilla left Washington and traveled north during the summer months to spend time with friends and relatives in Providence and Boston. "Utterly worn and exhausted," she was forbidden by her doctor to even talk about her school while traveling, though she found it impossible to comply. People constantly asked about the details of her work and her experiences in Washington, and the moment she felt the least bit better, she was meeting with potential donors and working to raise money for her school. Despite her weariness, she did her best to project strength. "She gave the impression from the first of great power,—mental, moral, and spiritual. . . . There was a sense of her being thoroughly alive," wrote one friend who visited with Myrtilla that summer.

Though she seemed to gain back some mental stability during her trip, her physical health still suffered. While traveling in New England, Myrtilla visited Harriet Beecher Stowe, who became alarmed at her frail appearance and immediately took charge of the situation. At Harriet's insistence, and with her

The Gleason Sanitarium in Elmira, New York, where Myrtilla took part in the water cure treatment. "I was a pitiable invalid," she told a friend. *Courtesy of Steele Memorial Library, Elmira, New York*

Water Cure

Mid-19th century medical practices included a technique called hydropathy—or water cure. For people who suffered with certain sicknesses or diseases for which no known medical treatment existed, the therapeutic application of water often promised relief. The technique involved the liberal use of hot and cold baths, showers, compresses, and general hydration to cleanse the body and cure ailments. Tracing its roots to ancient civilizations, the water cure first appeared in the United States in the 1840s, and by the time Myrtilla took her treatments at Elmira there were no less than 70 water cure facilities throughout the country. Adding to the popularity of hydropathy was the appearance of numerous books and journals on the subject touting its success. The *Water-Cure Journal*, a periodical devoted to the uses and application of hydropathy, enjoyed wide readership—including Myrtilla, who became a devoted believer in the technique. Though the water cure would ultimately fall into disuse as a practical treatment for disease, it survives today in the form of hydrotherapy for the treatment of muscle soreness and sports injuries.

doctors' blessing, Myrtilla was admitted to a therapeutic facility in Elmira, New York, called Gleason Sanitarium, which offered a popular "water cure" treatment. Through the fall and into the winter, she was treated daily with warm and cold baths, compresses, showers, and water-saturated blanket wraps, all designed to reset the body's natural balance, remove toxins, and restore health and vitality without medicine or surgery.

So vital was Myrtilla to the cause of African American education that Harriet paid all of her water cure expenses and kept careful track of her progress at Elmira. Myrtilla's school was in jeopardy, and Harriet would do everything she could to keep it going. "At present under God," she warned, "everything depends on you, therefore before everything take care of your health."

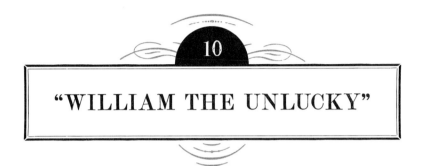

"WILLIAM THE UNLUCKY"

Myrtilla's scholars were greatly concerned about the health of their "invalid teacher," and despite the bitterness that had earlier developed about her strict and erratic behavior, they wrote warm letters to her while she was away and looked forward to her speedy recovery. While Myrtilla was in the North receiving treatments in the fall of 1855, Harriet hired Lydia B. Mann, the sister of the great educator Horace Mann, to temporarily run the School for Colored Girls in Myrtilla's absence.

Lydia appeared overwhelmed by the burdens of overseeing the school and wanted to make her stay in Washington, DC, a short one. She had left her job as superintendent of the Colored Female Orphan Asylum in Providence, Rhode Island, in order to help Myrtilla, and she was anxious to return to her post. A search for a suitable replacement proved unsuccessful, however, and in the spring of 1856, Myrtilla was forced to return to Washington and resume her teaching, though she was far from fully recovered. "I am quite well again except my poor brain, which

Lydia Mann

Horace Mann's sister Lydia shared her brother's love and enthusiasm for teaching. Born in 1798, two years after Horace, she began her teaching career in the district schools of Massachusetts and distinguished herself as a selfless and competent educator. Her clear abilities and friendly demeanor in the classroom were quickly noticed, and she was chosen to head the more challenging "winter schools" (classes held during the winter season) of her New England town. Soon Lydia found her calling as a teacher of African American orphans in Providence, Rhode Island. There she cared for, taught, and loved the children as if they were her own. Her affectionate and happy spirit brightened the sad plight of these disadvantaged young people. She was remembered by a commentator as "A True Woman,—Strong, Pure, Patient." She remained unmarried for her entire life and dedicated herself fully to the cause of her students.

will not work well more than three hours a day—nor three days in a week," she wrote.

While Myrtilla was still in New York, Samuel Rhoads had begun the work of creating a formal association to manage the school. Up until that time Samuel and Thomas Williamson personally owned the school property in an unofficial trust arrangement, and donations for construction of a new building were handled haphazardly and without any central command.

A change was necessary in order to manage the school's growth. In May 1856, the Philadelphia Friends and the Beecher family came together for this purpose to form the Washington Association for the Education of Free Colored Youth. Led by a distinguished panel of philanthropists, politicians, publishers, and abolitionists, the new organization, it was hoped, would become the chief authority in the school's management, handling all matters regarding its development and funding.

At Harriet's suggestion, another of her brothers, William H. Beecher, was named secretary of the association in charge of all marketing and fundraising.

William's appointment would prove to be a disaster.

——— •••• ———

In the Beecher family, William was affectionately known as "William the Unlucky." Unlike his overachieving siblings, it seemed that virtually everything William touched failed. Things would prove no different in his short-lived service to Myrtilla's school. Right from the start he was able to raise only enough money to cover his own expenses. His work schedule was sporadic, and to Myrtilla's irritation, his methods were often wasteful. In time his actions would turn downright dangerous.

In December 1856, William created his own edition of the annual circular that Myrtilla and others had developed to publicize her school and raise funds. Up until then all of the circulars had been carefully worded and discreetly issued so as not to raise the ire of Washington, DC, residents who might disapprove of Myrtilla's work. In promoting the school, it was important not to present it as something to be feared. William's version of the circular, however, went far beyond anything previously attempted.

William Beecher

Born on January 15, 1802, in New Haven, Connecticut, William Henry Beecher was the oldest son of Lyman Beecher and Roxana Foote. A poor student and a slow learner, William was destined to become one of the least-known and least-remembered Beechers. He lived under the shadow of his more successful and high-achieving siblings, failing at every instance to fulfill his potential. He began his working life as an apprentice cabinet-maker and store clerk but was frequently unhappy and aimless in his career path. He tried several other jobs, but on each occasion his efforts were met with failure. Following his father's lead he studied religion at Andover Theological Seminary but completed his course work only with his father's untiring assistance. William finally became a licensed preacher in 1830 and was appointed minister of his first parish in Newport, Rhode Island, but the assignment did not last long. With the help of family members he was placed, in the coming years, in a variety of churches across New England, New York, and Ohio, but every assignment seemed to end in some kind of dispute over money or personality. His work as a reverend at a North Brookfield, Massachusetts, church, however, lasted for nearly 20 years. Upon the death of his wife, Katherine, in 1870, William retired from the ministry and moved to Chicago to live with his children. Throughout his life he was a strong believer in the abolitionist movement. He died in June 1889.

In an innocent but ignorant blunder, he implied in his December circular that the School for Colored Girls would be available for students of color *beyond* the borders of Washington, DC, and that funds were sought for the construction of a new schoolhouse for that purpose. "There are in the United States *five hundred thousand* free people of color," he wrote. "There are [in Washington, DC] . . . *eleven thousand* of this suffering people . . . and . . . in the adjoining states of Maryland and Virginia, *one hundred and thirty thousand* equally destitute." Kicking off a fundraising effort in his home state of Massachusetts the following spring, William attended a meeting at the Tremont Temple in Boston and distributed to a group of local gentlemen—and newspaper reporters—promotional information stating that he was hoping to raise $20,000 "to erect a larger and more suitable edifice for the reception of . . . the numerous free blacks in the District *and adjacent States.*" The proposed building, he wrote, "is designed to accommodate 150 scholars and to furnish homes for the teachers and pupils from a distance." The message was unambiguous: Myrtilla's school was now actively seeking to attract and educate black students from not only the nation's capital but also the surrounding states.

On April 18, 1857, the *Boston Journal* published William's statement word for word. News traveled fast to the people of Washington, DC, and immediately new feelings of hostility began to fester in the city against Myrtilla and her efforts. Just a few weeks after the *Boston Journal* article came out, the former mayor Walter Lenox—the man who had signaled his support of Myrtilla's school when it first opened but then refused to meet with her—penned a scathing letter condemning the school in the Washington, DC, newspaper the *National Intelligencer.*

In an arrogant and inflated tirade that included a complete reprinting of William's circular as it had appeared in the *Boston*

Journal, Lenox denounced the School for Colored Girls as "an unjust and dangerous interference with the interests and feelings" of Washington, DC. "This scheme," he complained, "was started some years ago . . . and in the foothold it has already gained it feels secure of its future progress. Earnest, prompt action can now arrest it peacefully," he wrote. Then, in a threatening tone, he warned, "Tumult and blood may stain its future."

Lenox argued that Myrtilla's school would deluge the city with black students and their families, making it harder for white workers to find jobs while placing a greater burden on public services. "Justice to ourselves and kindness to them," he wrote, "require that we should prohibit immigration [of black families] and encourage their removal from our [city] limits."

He then claimed that the level of education Myrtilla provided to her African American students was, in essence, *too* good. "Is it, then, just to ourselves, or humane to the colored population, for us to permit a degree of instruction so far beyond their political and social condition . . . ?" he asked. Well-educated free African Americans, argued Lenox, would become restless and unhappy—and unwilling to "fill that position in society which is allotted to them."

He then attempted to make the issue one of national rather than just local importance. He accused the school of being an instrument in a much larger Northern abolitionist conspiracy to convert Washington, DC, into the "headquarters of 'slavery agitation,'" and as evidence he pointed to the well-known antislavery aims and objectives of the school's backers and supporters—all of whom were named in the circular. The secret goal of the school, claimed Lenox, was nothing short of the abolition of slavery. He appealed to Myrtilla's supporters to take the school up North and to leave the people of the South alone. "If your humanity demands this particular sphere for its action . . . ," he

Walter Lenox, the 13th mayor of Washington, DC. Seemingly a friend to the School for Colored Girls upon its opening, Lenox later turned on Myrtilla with a vicious attack in the *National Intelligencer.* *From the book, Walter Lenox, the Thirteenth Mayor, Allen C. Clark, Records of the Columbia Historical Society, Vol XX, 1917*

begged, "establish separate institutions in the free States . . . but do not seek to impose upon us a system contrary to our wishes and interests. . . . We must insist that within our limits we are the best, and must be the exclusive, judges of the character and degree of instruction that shall be imparted to this class of our population."

Then, seemingly placing on Myrtilla the fate of the nation and even the prospect of civil war, Lenox accused the school's "influence" of threatening to "rend asunder the 'Union itself.'" He ended his letter with an ominous warning to Myrtilla and her supporters if they chose to continue the school: "The responsibility will be with those who by their own wanton acts of aggression make resistance a necessity."

Lenox was, at the time, a highly respected "Christian gentleman" whose opinions on the issue of slavery and the teaching

of free black children were shared by an overwhelming majority of the "refined society" of Washington, DC—a city built on
freedom, liberty, and equality. As Ellen O'Connor later wrote,
Lenox's letter as it appeared in the *National Intelligencer* demonstrated "the high tide which pro-slavery feeling had reached,
when one of the most conservative and respectable of American
newspapers could open its columns for such an attack on one fee-
ble woman for teaching a few innocent girls to read and write."

———————◆———————

Almost a year before the Lenox letter appeared, Myrtilla had
once again left Washington, DC, for the soothing water cure
at Elmira, New York. Her health continued to be a problem,
and for the foreseeable future she felt incapable of returning to
her teaching duties at the school. She and Harriet frantically
searched for a substitute teacher, but the role was an uninvit-
ing one and no willing teacher was found. The school remained
closed for the rest of 1856 through the fall of 1857 while Myrtilla
regained her health and continued her fundraising efforts in the
North.

Lenox's letter, published while Myrtilla was still recovering
in New York, was reprinted in many newspapers and magazines
throughout the region and into the New England states. Even
in areas considered by most to be open-minded and tolerant
on the issue of slavery, the article generated much controversy
and anger against Myrtilla and her school. William Beecher,
the cause of the whole affair, admitted that the article ended all
possible fundraising efforts. "Ex-Mayor Lenox's letter appeared
just as we were opening our subscription and of course *killed*
it dead," he wrote. Soon after, William resigned from his position with the school, and the Washington Association for the

Education of Free Colored Youth was abandoned as a functioning organization. People associated with Myrtilla began experiencing angry reprisals for their support of the school, and one, Leonard Gale, who was mentioned in the article, was fired from his job at the United States Patent Office. The School for Colored Girls appeared to be headed for failure.

But Myrtilla would not give up. She hurried back to Washington as soon as her health permitted and rushed to the offices of Gales and Seaton, the editorial firm of the *National Intelligencer.* The distinguished and stately business was intimidating to Myrtilla, but nevertheless she stormed into the building and sternly asked the owner, William Seaton, if he could spare a moment. Escorted into his office, she scolded the gentleman, whom she later described as "a real old fogy," for endorsing Lenox's opinions, and she accused the editor of promoting underhanded and political motives against her school. The two argued and discussed the broader issues of slavery and the treatment of African Americans, but it was soon clear to Myrtilla that she could not change his mind and that no public apology would be offered by the editor. Instead, she returned to her school and recommitted herself to its success.

Unfolding national events, however, would soon make her job significantly more difficult.

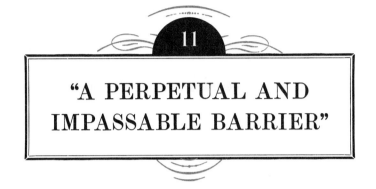

"A PERPETUAL AND IMPASSABLE BARRIER"

In March 1857, the US Supreme Court handed down a decision that would embolden proslavery Southerners like Walter Lenox and hasten America's path to civil war. The Dred Scott case, as it was called, declared that African Americans, whether free or enslaved, could not become US citizens. The very foundation of American liberty as stated in the Declaration of Independence that "all men are created equal" simply did not apply to what the court described as "that unfortunate race." In a shameful stain on the judicial system, and on the country itself, Chief Justice Roger B. Taney wrote that blacks were historically

regarded as beings of an inferior order, and altogether unfit to associate with the white race either in social or political relations, and so far inferior that they had no rights which the white man was bound to respect; and that the negro might justly and lawfully be reduced to slavery for his benefit. He was bought and sold and treated as an ordinary article of merchandise and traffic, whenever a profit could be made by it.

In finding that "a perpetual and impassable barrier was intended to be erected between the white race and the one which they had reduced to slavery," the Supreme Court concluded that African Americans were simply not entitled to any protections of the Constitution. Restrictions on slavery in all US territories were ended by the decision, effectively invalidating the Missouri Compromise, which for years had acted as a truce between North and South. Now, according to the court, slavery was a guaranteed right to any state that desired it.

The Dred Scott case ensured that, despite a brave woman's efforts to educate African Americans in Washington, DC—and the efforts of many others like her—the institution of slavery would end only at the point of a sword.

———◆———

Right about the time the Dred Scott decision reverberated across the country, Myrtilla reopened her school in Washington, DC. Still unable to assume full teaching responsibilities, she finally found someone willing to assist. A New York abolitionist Quaker named Emily Howland had met Myrtilla in Philadelphia the previous year and learned of her need for a substitute teacher. Like Myrtilla, Emily had a big heart and longed to lend a hand in a useful way. Though not a teacher by training, Emily took some courses and student-taught at some local schools, and in the fall of 1857 she traveled to Washington, DC, to work with Myrtilla.

It was now obvious to Myrtilla that the strains of running the school were far too demanding for her to handle, even with help. Her physical and mental health remained fragile, and it was clear that her role in the school had to change. After much encouragement she persuaded Emily to take on the lion's share

~~~~~~~~~~~~~~~~~~~~~~~~~~~~~~~~~~~~~~~

Dred Scott

In 1833 a US Army surgeon named John Emerson was transferred from his home state of Missouri to a military post in Illinois. Accompanying Emerson was his African American slave, Dred Scott. During the next five years the two men resided in Illinois and Wisconsin—both free states where slavery was not permitted. Living as a free man, Scott married in 1836, and two years later the couple voluntarily returned to Missouri shortly after Emerson's transfer back to the South, and there they remained until Emerson's death in 1840. In 1843 Emerson's widow attempted to sell or lease Dred Scott to another military officer. Unable to buy his own freedom, Scott brought a lawsuit claiming that his extended stay in several Northern free states meant that he was now legally a free man. The resulting decision of Chief Justice Roger B. Taney of the US Supreme Court, sealing Dred Scott's fate as an enslaved person, set back the cause of African American rights for years to come and heightened regional tensions in a prelude to the Civil War. Following the case, a politician from Missouri, Taylor Blow, purchased Scott together with his entire family and freed them in May 1857.

~~~~~~~~~~~~~~~~~~~~~~~~~~~~~~~~~~~~~~~

Emily Howland

Born in 1827 into a wealthy Quaker family near Sherwood, New York, Emily Howland from an early age adopted her parents' abolitionist and social reform convictions. Her father, Slocum, was an antislavery advocate and offered his family home as a way station on the Underground Railroad. As a child, Emily enrolled in several New York State boarding schools and in 1851 attended Margaret Robinson's School in Philadelphia. In the coming years she tutored classes and attended lectures while her interest in reform movements such as suffrage and education grew. After her teaching experience at Myrtilla's school in Washington, DC, Emily returned home to care for her ailing mother and to tend to household matters. During the Civil War she moved to Arlington, Virginia, where she taught formerly enslaved people to read and write. Frustrated with the lack of government support for African Americans after the war, Emily purchased 350 acres of land in Virginia with her father's help and settled formerly enslaved people on the property. At about the same time she founded the Howland Chapel School in Northumberland County, Virginia, for African American children. As word spread of Emily's good works, many local citizens requested that she create and fund other school projects. Upon her father's death in 1881, she gave generously of his estate to the cause of African American education. In 1890 Emily became the first woman director of a national bank. She lived to the age of 101.

Abolitionist and teacher Emily Howland. While Myrtilla recovered from illness and tended to other interests, Emily took over duties at the School for Colored Girls. *Courtesy of Friends Historical Library of Swathmore College, PA-115*

of responsibility at the school, while she herself took on less and less. "Miss Howland is a host in herself, acting as house-keeper, teacher, scribe, and prophet," she wrote. "I serve simply as prompter general." In no condition to handle day-to-day teaching activities, Myrtilla quietly faded into a less active role, focusing instead on overall strategy and policy.

By the start of 1858 Myrtilla once again left Washington and traveled north to resume raising funds for the construction of her schoolhouse. She maintained that the existing buildings on the property were "pioneer-like" and much too run-down for her needs, and she used their poor condition as the basis for her pleas. Despite her fragile state, she journeyed through Massachusetts and New York, making her case for donations in churches and at abolitionist rallies, endlessly fighting a hacking cough and poor health. On February 10 she visited the author James Freeman Clarke with the result, "aside from my exhaustion," of a $100 donation. She collected $900 in Boston with a promise of $1,000 more in the near future, and she sought donations again from Henry Ward Beecher and the farmer and abolitionist Titus Chapin.

"I have walked myself so lame," she wrote in a letter to Emily, "many days I can scarcely move when night comes, and, sometimes, not even sit up or talk." Painfully aware of the problems generated by William Beecher's ill-fated 1856 circular, Myrtilla and her Northern friends worked to generate a new, less offensive marketing plan that she hoped to use in her efforts. Her work met with some success, and slowly she raised money, though the amount was well short of her goals.

Though her mind and body were focused on her fundraising campaign, Myrtilla's heart remained with her students and the work that Emily was so diligently continuing in Washington, DC. Myrtilla often wrote to Emily reminding her of chores and cleaning that needed to be done around the school buildings, and she suggested essay topics for the students to write about. When visitors to the school were expected, Myrtilla fretted in her typically obsessive manner: "I am anxious you should all appear clean and neat, with bodies washed and heads combed, orderly and quiet in manners; and the house in perfect order, ornamented with spring flowers."

Meanwhile, Emily concluded that she too needed help running the school. As Myrtilla had found, the burdens of maintaining the buildings and teaching the students alone were overwhelming, and so Emily recruited a former student of the school, Emma Brown, to lend a hand. Together, Emily and Emma successfully carried on the work of the school even in the face of simmering criticism generated by the *National Intelligencer* article and the racist mindset of the Dred Scott decision.

By the spring of 1858 the school had grown to nearly 60 students and even the kitchen had been modified into a makeshift classroom. The steady stream of curious visitors continued, among them a number of Quakers from Great Britain who showed great interest in the education of African Americans and the abolition of slavery as a whole. Emily and Emma remained politically aware on matters affecting the school and even visited Congress to listen to the speeches of senators and representatives about issues of the day.

Emily soon found the pressures of running the school to be more than she could take. She lost her appetite and became nervous and irritable. In need of rest, she temporarily left the school in June 1858, entrusting it to Emma's able care for the remainder of the term. Emma happily remained at the property through the summer and reopened the school to students in the fall.

In the North, though fundraising remained sluggish, Myrtilla was raising awareness of her cause. Even the former president Millard Fillmore, whom Myrtilla had not so gently scolded for ignoring her requests for a meeting at the Executive Mansion in 1851, now took notice. "I have made frequent inquiries to the success of the school," he wrote in a letter to her, "and I regard the cause as a benevolent one and entitled to the patronage and material aid of all charitable persons." She could only wish that money flowed in as easily as the praise.

That summer Emily regained her strength and made a formal agreement with Myrtilla to take over complete control of the school until Myrtilla was able to resume her teaching duties. Emily, it was decided, was free to carry out any teaching plans she wished without interference from Myrtilla—though ultimate ownership of the school would remain with its founder.

In November 1858, a rested and revitalized Emily returned to Washington, DC, with a new assistant, her friend Anna Searing, and resumed her authority from Emma. With Myrtilla's help, Emma would go on to Oberlin College to further her education as a teacher, but not before opening her own small schoolroom in the Georgetown section of Washington, DC. Emily continued her capable management of the school's growing number of students and believed, through good and bad, that her efforts and the devotion of her scholars "could kindle a fire which should light this whole nation."

Though the management of the school was in good hands, its *legal* status continued to haunt Myrtilla. She felt constantly threatened by Samuel Rhoads and Thomas Williamson, who still held official title to the property, and she continued to press for the creation of an association or other independent organization to take ownership, since she herself could not realistically do so. She feared that if her relationship with the Philadelphia Quakers completely broke down—or if the men died—she would be left with no personal right to the property. She would, in essence, be excluded from her own school. Unfortunately, her lawyers informed her that an organization formed for the purpose of teaching African Americans would surely be rejected by Washington, DC, courts as a public nuisance and be disbanded as soon as it was created.

Myrtilla also remained frustrated by the trustees' unwillingness to move forward with construction of the new schoolhouse. She had been only marginally successful in her fundraising efforts. Thousands of dollars needed for the building still remained either unpledged or uncollected, but this did not stop Myrtilla. She insisted that construction should begin anyway. In a series of letters to Samuel she rudely accused him of standing in the way of the school's progress and demanded that he allow work on the building to begin immediately. He patiently and correctly pointed out that until the *full* amount of funds necessary for the construction were donated the trustees could not agree to move forward. To do so would leave the school—and the trustees—in debt without a way to get out.

Myrtilla was unmoved. She thought the Philadelphians were entirely too conservative, and she complained bitterly about what she considered to be unjust and unreasonable obstruction of progress. Angered and feeling betrayed by the men, she set out to find new trustees who would act more boldly on her vision. In 1859, after enduring months of eccentric badgering from Myrtilla, Samuel finally reached the end of his patience and agreed to relinquish control. Myrtilla had managed to destroy her strongest and most dedicated alliance. Totally frustrated, Samuel informed her that "any further correspondence must therefore be confined to this single point." He made it clear that he was through with her.

The question of who would serve as trustee and take ownership of the property remained unanswered for more than a year while Myrtilla consulted with and often insulted and antagonized her business associates. The goal of constructing a new schoolhouse dominated her thoughts, and it was plain that she would do anything—even sacrifice friendships—to achieve her ambition. As the search for new allies continued, she worked tirelessly in the North to raise funds and awareness for her cause.

Seven years had passed since the School for Colored Girls had opened, and though Myrtilla had removed herself from teaching, she remained deeply proud of the fact that a number of her graduates had gone on to become teachers themselves. "It is pleasant to see the harvest gathered during one's life time," she wrote.

Emma Brown, living proof of that harvest, remained eternally grateful to Myrtilla for allowing her the opportunity to pass on her legacy of education. "If I teach others although it may be ever so little, and they teach succeeding generations," Emma wrote to Myrtilla, "your good work will be increased and in this way *only* I feel that I can repay you for all your kind teaching."

THIS NOBLE WOMAN

Emily Howland was a dedicated leader at the school. She formed close relationships with the students and taught them that their ultimate responsibility was to learn all they could in order to free the world of slavery. Every week she issued to the students a written critique that reviewed both the "excellencies and defects" of the class and urged the girls to earnest and noble aims. Sometimes the critiques were long, involved lectures, but on occasion they contained scathing rebukes of poor behavior. Though challenged and often exhausted by her efforts, Emily found the job rewarding, and she enjoyed the independence that Myrtilla had given her.

In February 1859 Myrtilla abruptly returned to Washington without even a message or advance notice and made it perfectly clear to Emily who was in charge of the School for Colored Girls. She "popped catlike upon us," wrote a frustrated Emily in a letter home. Myrtilla's angry and unpredictable side seemed to have returned with her arrival, and the two no doubt engaged in a heated argument over who would be running the school. Immediately their relationship crumbled, and Emily moved from the house. She had been promised full control of the school without interference, but now Myrtilla once again exerted her critical and often unreasonable influence. Within a month, Emily left Washington, DC. "I have told M. Miner that I will never live with her again," she wrote.

The quarrel between the two women caused a stir in Washington social circles and again revealed Myrtilla's volatile and ill-tempered side. Most believed that she had forced Emily from the school with her abrasive and abrupt personality, but Myrtilla insisted that she was simply misunderstood and that her actions should be excused because of her emotional frailties. Her friends were less forgiving. They blamed Emily's departure on Myrtilla's unruly temper, and they predicted that the school could not prosper with Myrtilla in charge alone. Even Emma Brown hesitatingly admitted, "I do not like or respect Miss M. I know this is wrong, but I cannot help feeling so, or explain my feelings."

Without Emily's assistance, the school began to decline. Another former student, Matilda Jones, took over most of the teaching responsibilities while Myrtilla focused her attentions elsewhere. Her fascination with spiritualism and the occult that had begun years earlier now became obsessive, and she seemed to lose interest in her school. It was as if her heart was no longer in her work as an educator; she even began selling sewing machines on the side to supplement her income.

Soon, enrollment began to fall and the school's reputation faltered. "We understand that the colored people are getting very much dissatisfied and that all of the best scholars are leaving the school," wrote one Washington observer. Soon even those close to Myrtilla thought that she had in fact closed her doors.

As the school deteriorated, so too did the political climate in the United States. On October 16, 1859, a militant abolitionist named John Brown led a raid upon the federal weapons arsenal at Harpers Ferry, Virginia, hoping to arm Southern slaves and spark a general rebellion. The attempt failed but enraged sentiments on both sides of the now growing conflict. The issue of slavery was tearing the nation apart, and war seemed more likely than ever.

Aware of the importance of her school, Myrtilla fought the impulse to quit and carried on. After a months-long search for an acceptable trustee to take ownership of the school property on her behalf and manage construction of a new building, a New York businessman and old friend of Myrtilla's, Benjamin Tatham, finally stepped in. Samuel Rhoads and Thomas Williamson gladly gave Benjamin a deed to the property and handed over all moneys that had been collected for the school—about $3,000.

With the country on the brink of war, political and racial tensions soared in Washington, DC, and across the nation, and donations for African American education all but dried up, as did any rational notion of constructing a new schoolhouse. Potential donors—and the public at large—simply had no stomach for any activities that might further infuriate regional passions. But Myrtilla refused to give up. Though her school was in decline, she continued to believe it could be revived with a new and well-planned building. In typical fashion she battled with Benjamin, insisting that he release funds and begin construction. It was not to be.

In the moonlit early morning hours of May 13, 1860, Myrtilla awoke to the sound of flames crackling around her. A fire had

John Brown

Among American abolitionists, perhaps none was as radical in his beliefs as John Brown. Born in 1800 into a devoutly religious family, Brown was taught by his father and community of the evils of slavery. He married twice and had 20 children, and spent most of his years moving from state to state working various jobs to support his growing family. Though he was unsuccessful in business and financially poor, he still managed to support abolitionist causes. In his later years he became more militant in his antislavery views and advocated violence to accomplish his goals. In 1855 he moved to the Kansas Territory and became a fighter in the battle to stop the western spread of slavery. As a self-appointed leader, Brown commanded a small company in an attack against five proslavery men and boys in Pottawatomie Creek, ruthlessly killing all of them. Later, he led a raid against a Missouri slaveholder, freeing 11 enslaved people and murdering their master. Believing that his actions were justified as God's will, Brown continued his radical activities and soon became a hero to many in the abolitionist movement. In 1859 he put into action his long-planned scheme to start a slave rebellion. With 21 armed accomplices, he attacked the federal arsenal at Harper's Ferry, Virginia, and though he was able to occupy the fort for a short while, he was quickly overrun by federal troops and arrested. Convicted of treason, John Brown was hanged on December 2, 1859.

been intentionally set in the school building that served as her home, threatening her life and all that she had worked for. She rushed to the front window, screaming for help in an "awful fury," then ran for water to douse the flames.

Neighbors heard her screams, and one of them quickly scrambled to the roof of the building and smothered the fire there. Rushing back to her bedroom, Myrtilla found her curtains and some scrap papers ablaze. With the help of fellow citizens, the fire was mercifully put out and her school buildings were saved. The same, however, could not be said for Myrtilla's resolve.

The fire was symbolic of the country itself and of the constant threat to Myrtilla's quest. She had given her heart and soul to the education of African Americans. She had angered many and at times isolated herself in gloom, but she stayed true to her cause. She had taken bold action when others warned against it, and she accomplished what they said could never be done. But now, as she stood amid the smoldering remains of her school building, Myrtilla gathered her thoughts and wondered if she could endure another moment. As Ellen O'Connor later wrote, "The shadows of the approaching conflict were deepening on the horizon; the blasts of opposition were so fierce, the elements on every hand were so threatening, that, in her shattered health, she felt incapable of breasting the storm which she had long known must come sooner or later."

———◆◆———

On November 6, 1860, a tall and gangly country lawyer from Springfield, Illinois, named Abraham Lincoln was elected 16th president of the United States. A member of the antislavery Republican Party, Lincoln was swept into office with a considerable majority despite not having the support of a single Southern state. Within weeks of the election, seven proslavery Southern states seceded from the Union, and the rest soon followed. Their goal was to create a new country—the Confederate States of America—where slavery could continue without Northern interference. The move led directly to the Civil War.

Secession

Prior to the Civil War, the cultural, political, and economic divide between the Northern and Southern states was virtually insurmountable. The South's labor-driven agricultural society had grown farther and farther apart from the industrialized cities of the North, and slavery had driven a wedge between these two cultures. The election of Abraham Lincoln as president of the United States was the final straw. Lincoln believed that the spread of slavery into the western territories should be stopped, and this infuriated those in the South who depended heavily on slave labor. Many Southerners believed that their very way of life was being threatened by Northern interference. On December 20, 1860, South Carolina seceded from the Union—removing itself from the laws and government of the United States. In the coming months, 11 more Southern states seceded to form a new and separate country called the Confederate States of America. Led by its newly elected president, Jefferson Davis, this renegade nation established its capital in Richmond, Virginia.

After the fire at her school, Myrtilla decided that she needed a change in scenery, and she left Washington, DC, for the Midwest, where she continued selling sewing machines for a living. Benjamin Tatham, Emily Howland, and others continued their interest in the school and attempted to keep it running during her absence, but no permanent teacher could be found to take things over.

Even prior to her departure, Myrtilla's important legacy was beginning to be understood. In a contentious debate in the US Senate regarding the proposed use of public funds to educate African Americans in the District of Columbia, Henry Wilson, a senator from Natick, Massachusetts, and future vice president of the United States, rose to the Senate floor and proclaimed, "There is a noble woman here in Washington teaching colored girls; and if [opposing senators] visited that school and saw the

mental culture there, if they would not be proud of it, and thank God that these darkened minds were being cultivated . . . I misunderstand those gentlemen altogether."

Henry Wilson, senator from Massachusetts and 18th vice president of the United States. *McClees & Beck, Prints & Photographs Division, Library of Congress, LC-DIG-ppmsca-26560*

From the moment of Lincoln's election the country prepared for war. Both the North and South fortified their vital positions, stockpiled their weapons, and readied their armies. On April 12, 1861, Confederate artillery opened fire on Fort Sumter, a stronghold of the federal government in the harbor of Charleston, South Carolina, after a rejected demand for surrender. It was the first shot of the Civil War—a war that would last for the next four years and claim over 600,000 American lives. The "grand conflict," as Myrtilla called it, would serve, she hoped, to "overthrow tyranny and establish universal Liberty . . . [and] secure to all men and women, of every nation, tribe, and people equal rights and privileges. Yours shall be as mine and mine as all others."

———•◆•———

In the spring of 1861, just as the war began, Myrtilla returned to Washington, DC, to wrap up the affairs of the school and prepare for a much longer trip west. Still the capital of the country and now the center of military logistics for the North, the city had become an urban fortress and the focal point of the Union war effort. Washington, wrote Myrtilla, "immediately assumed the appearance of a beleaguered city."

She met with friends and, despite the perils faced in the nation's capital during wartime, remained for a while to see if she could help nurse the wounded before she left the city. She attended the first reception for the new president at the Executive Mansion, and though she was not able to personally greet him in the throng of well-wishers, she did see him. "[I] stood near Mr. Lincoln a long time," she wrote to her brother. "His face is much better than any engraving of him I have seen & I like his appearance decidedly."

Several days later, she stored all of the school's books, maps, and supplies in one of its buildings and turned over the property to renters. Bidding good-bye to the School for Colored Girls for

~~~~~~

United States Civil War

Lasting four years and taking more than 600,000 American lives, the Civil War was without question the darkest and most perilous period in the nation's history. After the first shots fired at Fort Sumter, the war spread across the South in a series of bloody and savage battles designed to capture land and eliminate or cripple armies. The First Battle of Bull Run, the first major land battle of the war, occurred on July 21, 1861, near Manassas, Virginia, and resulted in about 3,000 Union (Northern) casualties and over 1,700 Confederate (Southern) casualties. Bull Run proved that the Civil War would be a long and bloody conflict. The Battle of Gettysburg alone, which lasted three long days in the summer of 1863, resulted in the death, wounding, or capture of nearly 51,000 men—but neither side could truly claim victory. It took two more years of brutal conquest for the North to defeat Jefferson Davis and his Confederate states. The American Civil War ended officially on April 9, 1865, when Southern general Robert E. Lee surrendered his decimated army to Northern general Ulysses S. Grant, thereby ending the Southern dream of a separate country where slave labor was allowed and encouraged.

~~~~~~

the last time, Myrtilla traveled north to Philadelphia, where she began her journey to a new life.

———◆———

Shortly after Achsa's death in 1850, Myrtilla had become interested in the spirit world. Searching for comfort in her grief, she attempted to communicate with her deceased sister through the help of a spirit medium. At the time, belief in spiritualism and the occult was sweeping the nation. Lecturers and seers, as they were called, claimed the certainty of life after death and even mind over matter, and suggested that visions, trances, and séances might bring spiritual enlightenment and knowledge even beyond religion. Over 1.5 million Americans participated in the spiritualist movement, the center of which began in Myrtilla's home state of New York.

Myrtilla came to believe that she could look into the future and even heal the sick. She claimed that she could contact spirits of the dead, and she attempted to read the contents of letters through mental telepathy simply by placing them to her forehead. She became an avid supporter of phrenology, the claimed ability to determine personality characteristics from skull shape, and of healing through magnetism, the manipulation of magnetic impulses in the body. Demonstrating the impressionable nature of her personality, she consulted with a spiritualist who placed a letter written by Myrtilla's friend, a Mrs. Gale, to her forehead and provided a "reading" of the writer's personality.

"This person does not look back, but lives in the present and in the future, not in the past," said the entranced seer. "An aspiring, grasping person, aiming at something beyond reach, hungering and thirsting for something great and good—for knowledge—ever pressing on and on, with no time to look

Spiritualism

Closely related to the religious and reform movements originating in New York State's Burned-Over District, the idea of spiritualism—or communication with the spirits of the dead—became a widely held belief in mid-19th-century America. The spiritualist movement began on March 31, 1848, when two young girls, Kate and Margaretta Fox, claimed to a neighbor that they had heard a series of ghostly rapping sounds on the walls and furnishings of their Hydesville, New York, bedroom. Later, in the presence of onlookers, the sisters seemed to communicate with what appeared to be an unearthly entity that responded to questions with sequential knocks that indicated intelligent direction. Though years later they admitted that their spirit contact had been nothing more than an elaborate hoax, the Fox sisters became a national sensation. At the time, the Rochester area of New York where the girls lived was a center of religious and reform activity, and the people were particularly receptive to the possibility of communication with the spirit world. The press widely reported on the Fox sisters, and soon spiritualist beliefs swept the area. Mediums claiming the ability to channel the spirits of the departed advertised their gifts, and bereaved relatives lined up for the chance to make contact with dead family members through séances. By 1880 it was said that an estimated eight million people in Europe and the United States considered themselves spiritualists. Though many even today believe in the spirit world, the movement seemed to fade as more and more mediums and spiritual episodes were exposed as hoaxes.

back." Missing the generality of the statement and its applicability to almost everyone, Myrtilla was struck with awe: "How this stranger could come to this knowledge with no preconsciousness of Mrs. Gale's existence is to me another of the mysteries of mind and its wonderful powers."

Some of Myrtilla's friends had also become spiritual believers, but many others scoffed at the idea. Her obsession with the occult often interfered with her business relationships and no doubt contributed to the decline of her school. Sayles J. Bowen, a businessman and one of Myrtilla's most ardent supporters in the past, now mockingly wrote to Emily Howland, "If the spirits can so far control her as to cause her to govern her temper and that loose unruly [mouth] of hers properly, the world will have lost nothing when they take the guardianship of her." Clearly, he thought Myrtilla had lost her mind.

After closing her school she traveled west and settled in San Francisco, California, where she intended to relax and regain her health. As ever she had very little money and needed to find a way to support herself. Weary of the teaching profession, she turned toward her spiritual abilities in order to earn a living. She advertised in local newspapers her powers as a "Magnetic Physician":

CITIZENS FRIENDS

M. Miner from Washington, D.C., comes to you endowed with that remarkable power of Sympathetic Clairvoyance which enables her to discover the causes of Disease and apply the remedy. Diseases which evade all other modes of examination and yield to no other system of treatment, are clearly revealed to the Sympathetic Clairvoyant, and easily brought under control; while Diseases in all their forms, physical and mental, chronic and acute, are alike subject to its power, relying as it does on Nature's great remedial agents, Water, Air, and Magnetism.

Her advertisements, posting regular office hours, insisted that nearly everyone has the gift of "animal magnetism" and she could reveal that gift to "alleviate pain and exterminate disease." She claimed that mothers especially should learn these methods to "save their children from premature death."

Myrtilla seemed to find happiness in California with a slower pace and less stressful lifestyle. "The angels guide me very definitely each day," she wrote to her brother in New York. She earned enough money with her clairvoyant "powers" to get by in California and even sent Benjamin Tatham, her trustee, $200 to be used for the restoration of her school in Washington, DC.

Though she remained committed to the goal of African American education, she no longer saw herself as useful to the cause. "Having done what I could to role [*sic*] that ball I rest in peace," she wrote. She knew that at some point she would return to Washington, but she was unsure of what her work would be. The uncertainties of war made future plans difficult, but Myrtilla remained very optimistic that the work for racial equality would continue—with or without her.

———•———

She was right. Though she was no longer actively involved with the School for Colored Girls, others remained very interested in the cause. Emily Howland continued to correspond with Myrtilla's sponsors, and even Ednah Thomas—the woman who had provided Myrtilla with her first donation of $100 back in 1851—asked about the school's status. Soon supporters and friends began thinking of ways to revive it. Myrtilla had laid the foundation for its ultimate success; all that was lacking was the proper means to achieve the goal.

Her old associate Sayles Bowen began talking to people in Washington, DC, about restoring the school, and he hoped that Lydia Mann, Anna Searing, and Emily Howland, all former teachers at the school, could now reunite to operate it. Sayles refused to be personally named in the effort because of his disdain for Myrtilla, but he believed in the cause and insisted that the three women were the perfect teachers. "You three have the confidence and good will of the entire population here, white and colored," he told Emily, "and Miss [Miner] is obnoxious to all." No matter his opinions of Myrtilla, the work would have to be approved by the existing trustee of the school, Benjamin Tatham, who in turn was obligated to consult with Myrtilla before anything could be done. Sayles was not optimistic. "Her majesty," as he sarcastically called Myrtilla, was very unpredictable and, at present, far removed from Washington, DC. The exact details would have to wait until "the 'spirits' move her to return from California," he informed Emily.

Despite the complex details of administration, a political movement soon emerged to legally revive Myrtilla's school once and for all. With many Southern states no longer sending representatives to the US Congress during the Civil War, antislavery laws could be passed with much less opposition. It was finally time to provide the School for Colored Girls with a federal charter—a license of sorts—issued by Congress to carry on the work of educating African Americans.

———•—•———

On January 1, 1863, President Abraham Lincoln signed the Emancipation Proclamation effectively freeing three million

The Emancipation Proclamation

"I never, in my life, felt more certain that I was doing right, than I do in signing this paper," Abraham Lincoln said of the Emancipation Proclamation. "If my name ever goes into history it will be for this act, and my whole soul is in it." An exercise of the president's war powers under the Constitution, the Emancipation Proclamation was not only the morally right thing to do but also the militarily strategic thing to do. The Confederate government supported its army through the Southern economy—which was driven by slavery. In an attempt to deny the South its manpower, Lincoln justified the legality of emancipating the enslaved workers. In reality, however, a signature on a proclamation did not free a single person. It would take a Union victory in the Civil War to enforce the proclamation since the Southern states would never voluntarily give up the institution of slavery, but any person who could escape from a Southern slaveholder during the war was considered free. The proclamation resulted in the Union army's recruitment of thousands of formerly enslaved men, and for the duration of the war many African Americans bravely fought and died on American battlefields to end slavery once and for all. After the Civil War, Congress passed—and three quarters of the states ratified—the Thirteenth Amendment to the Constitution, which forever abolished slavery in the United States, an act that began with Lincoln's Emancipation Proclamation.

enslaved people. Though it would take over two more years of devastating warfare and a constitutional amendment to bring the act to full consequence, Lincoln had finally rebuked what

Abraham Lincoln, 16th president of the United States, signs the Emancipation Proclamation on January 1, 1863. *McClees & Beck, Prints & Photographs Division, Library of Congress, LC-DIG-pga-08283*

had come to be known as our "peculiar institution" once and for all.

A month later, against this backdrop, Senator Henry Wilson introduced a proposal to the US Senate, conceived by Myrtilla's friends and supporters, called "A Bill to incorporate the Institution for the Education of Colored Youth in the District of Columbia." The purpose of the measure was to give Myrtilla's school legally recognized permanent existence. In support of the bill Senator Lot M. Morrill from Maine rose and said, "I trust that from this time forth it will never occur in the Congress of the United States that it is thought proper or expedient to raise an objection against private individuals educating the negro if they choose to do so." The measure passed by a vote of 29 to 9, and on March 3, 1863, President Lincoln signed it into law. The Institution for the Education of Colored Youth of the District of Columbia was now, in the words of the law, free "to educate and improve the moral and intellectual condition of such of the colored youth of the nation as may be placed under its care and influence." Myrtilla's school, whether successfully operating or not—and no matter who managed its affairs or ran its classes in the future—would now be recognized by the power of the US government.

———————

Though Myrtilla was named in the new law as the school's founder and appointed as one of its directors, it was as if she were oblivious to the fact. Seemingly unconcerned by the momentous events occurring in Washington, DC, and on the battlefields of the east, Myrtilla, now 48 years old, gleefully toured Northern California with a company of friends. She traveled by steamboat from her home in San Francisco upriver to the state capital of Sacramento, where she boarded a stagecoach and journeyed north to the town of Marysville. From there she endured an 80-mile trek over rough and dusty trails by covered wagon—and then another 30 miles on the back of a mule into the Sierra Nevada. "One thing is certain," she wrote cheerfully to a friend in Boston:

> I am carried about this country to see and enjoy its magnificent scenery in a most remarkable manner, without any care or expense, save my time and talents, which pay for all. . . . I had the joy of finding my little mule surefooted over the snowy, rocky trail, so frightful that not a man of all the seven in our company dared ride down it; but I kept my seat, and got safe through. Some of the way the snow was four feet deep over the trail . . . and my poor mule slipped his hind feet entirely under him, and slid thus some yards. . . . This was while we were passing at the foot of Pilot Peak, one of the highest peaks of all the Sierras. Then we were on rocky, narrow, stair-like steeps, where the least false step of the mule would have thrown us into interminable depths. We passed over three of these immense heights, one of which took us down a continuous, very steep, zigzag trail of four miles, down, down, fearfully down, to the river, over rocks and rough foot-bridges,—no wagon road,—and then again up, up the mountain sides beyond, till I was all chafed and mauled and pummeled, so that I could not move without groaning for pain for many days and nights, but was *glad* all the time.

In the exhilaration of her travels through the scenic beauty of the Northwest, it seemed that Myrtilla had finally found the peace and happiness that had eluded her for years in Washington, DC.

———◆———

In 1829 future president of the United States Martin Van Buren reportedly wrote, "The Almighty certainly never intended that people should travel at such breakneck speed," referring to the coming railroad system. Van Buren's claim would be quoted over and over as the senseless rambling of a man stuck in the past and afraid of adventure. Myrtilla, on the other hand, had always loved the excitement of travel and the thrill of speed. She enjoyed riding fast horses and being swiftly transported in carriages over rough terrain. Even as a child she had watched as ponies trotted through the streets of her hometown, and she had imagined them sprinting hard with herself at the reigns. But it was Myrtilla's love of speed that finally stopped her in her tracks.

On May 8, 1864, she accompanied a friend in Petaluma, California, on a buggy ride drawn by a team of sleek black ponies. "I entered it with much exhilaration of feeling, for I greatly enjoy fast driving," she wrote. The ponies, driven hard by the coachman, swiftly galloped down the road with the buggy bobbing and dancing behind them. Myrtilla was delighted by the movement and sensations and, no doubt, urged her driver on. To her dismay, however, the road suddenly banked into two quick corners, and in an attempt to negotiate the turns, the buggy pitched hard and tumbled from the road. Myrtilla was thrown 30 feet into the air, "falling with a crash" and landing "with greatest force" on her right side.

With a bruised and injured hip, she was sent back to San Francisco, where she was forced to remain in bed for weeks.

The lack of movement upset her very much and soon resulted in terrible sickness. Her lungs filled with fluid and fever racked her body. Finally a "profuse hemorrhage of the right lung" brought her near death.

Myrtilla fought through the illness and recovered at least enough to leave her bed. Hobbling about the house on a cane and feeling poorly, her spirits were low and the happiness that she had found in California seemed to dissolve. "I was full of courage and ready for anything, as agile and strong as ever in my life," she wrote. "This has greatly changed me. . . . I am now very, very weak." It was time, she decided, to go home.

The trip east required a lengthy sea voyage by steamship from San Francisco along the Pacific coast to Mexico and into Central America; then a perilous land-trek across the small country of Panama (before construction of the Panama Canal) and boarding another ship on the far side of the isthmus for the final journey north. Myrtilla's trip took nearly two months and, in her weakened condition, nearly killed her.

She arrived in New York in August 1864 and stayed with friends for several months trying to regain her health. It was not to be. Her lungs were overcome with infection, and she was pummeled by a hacking cough that shook her body and burned to the core. The effects of untreated tuberculosis that plagued her for much of her life now made simply breathing almost impossible. And yet, though her condition worsened, Myrtilla talked of future plans and believed that she would one day recover. More than anything she wanted to return to Washington, DC, perhaps in the belief that she could once again be of some service to her fellow man. In December "a dying woman," as one account described her, was placed on a train bound for the nation's capital.

Staying at the home of her friend Nancy Johnson, who had assisted with the congressional charter of the Institution for the Education of Colored Youth, Myrtilla fell into a state of fever-induced confusion. She blissfully conversed with invisible friends as if they were right there in the room with her, and she often lapsed into periods of incoherent babble. When she could rationally talk without bouts of coughing, she met with friends—including Ellen O'Connor, who, saddened by Myrtilla's worsening condition, sat at her bedside and tended to her needs. Ellen listened patiently to Myrtilla's rambling statements and loyally replied to her letters.

Myrtilla died on December 17, 1864, at age 49. No fanfare accompanied her death. Several local newspapers acknowledged her passing, but little mention was made of her life's work or legacy. She was buried by grieving friends at the Oak Hill Cemetery in Washington, DC, in a grave unmarked by a memorial stone.

Fifteen years later, Henry Wilson, former senator and vice president of the United States, wrote of Myrtilla:

> There is something touchingly impressive in the life and purpose of Miss Miner. To the great and grim tragedy of human affairs they afford a delightful episode. In this selfish world,—with its grasping, jostling throng,—she seemed like some angel . . . on her mission of mercy. On the dark background of the nation's history it seemed an illuminated picture, resplendent with truthfulness and love. Her life of romantic incident was at once redolent and beautiful. It was in itself a sweet poem, a living evangel of a heart yearning toward humanity and filled with a sublime trust in God.

Though for years Myrtilla's tomb would remain unmarked and neglected, she would not be forgotten. Long after her death a formerly enslaved person recalling Myrtilla's work suggested that a suitable monument be provided to memorialize her life. Inscribed upon it, he aptly proposed, should be the words:

MYRTILLA MINER
Within this lowly grave a conqueror lies.

EPILOGUE

——•◆•——

"YOU ARE THAT MONUMENT"

The Institution for the Education of Colored Youth as authorized by Congress struggled in its infancy to fulfill its promise. During the Civil War the school property was seized by the US government and converted into a hospital for formerly enslaved people, thus preventing its original and intended use. The war effort had consumed much time and energy from the American people, and upon Myrtilla's death the directors had still reached no agreement as to who would run the school. Education of African Americans was simply not a high priority—even after the school was granted a charter. With the Northern victory in the Civil War and changing racial attitudes, however, it ultimately became very clear that Washington, DC, would need a teacher training school for African Americans.

In February 1871 Myrtilla's school merged into the education department of Howard University and reopened its doors with moneys raised by the Institution for the Education of Colored Youth. Shortly thereafter the school property that Myrtilla had worked so hard to purchase in 1853 for $4,300—the property that she sometimes defended with her life—was sold for $40,000, nearly ten times the original price. The astounding rise in real estate values in Washington, DC, and the resulting profitable sale ensured an annual income on the invested money and gave birth to the Miner Fund—a charitable organization in Myrtilla's name dedicated to African American education. In future years the fund would provide cash grants for the growth and maintenance of approved schools, support of educational projects, and the awarding of scholarships to worthy students.

The relationship with Howard University ended in 1877 when the school directors purchased a new property on 17th and Church Streets NW in Washington, DC, and constructed a large, beautiful new building using funds from the sale of Myrtilla's original property. The new school was named the Miner Normal School and was devoted to training African American teachers. Among the several invited guests at the school's dedication ceremony was Frederick Douglass, who in a moving speech recounted how Myrtilla had come to him for advice in 1851—and how she bravely moved forward with her plans even after his stern warnings. William Henry Channing, a longtime supporter of Myrtilla who also attended the event, later wrote, "If Myrtilla Miner's spirit was permitted to be present at the opening festival of her 'Normal School,' she must have felt herself blessed beyond her highest hope by such a marvelous triumph."

In 1887 the Miner Normal School became part of the public school system of Washington, DC. The students' education would at long last be funded by tax dollars and not just private donations. Over the coming years the school would develop into "an institution which offered its students a sound preparation for the profession of teaching . . . [and] stressed lofty ideals of character and appreciation for beauty as well as academic standards and practice in teaching." Myrtilla's school gained a national reputation for excellence in education.

In 1919 the school moved to a new location on Georgia Avenue and 10 years later changed its name to Miner Teachers College. By an act of Congress in 1929 the school became a four-year teaching institution of higher education. New courses in educational theory were added to the curriculum, and a student-teaching program was introduced to provide budding teachers with practical classroom experience. Over time the faculty increased to 55 members and the student body enrollment rose to over 600. With money donated by the Miner Fund, a library of more than 37,000 volumes was added to Miner Teachers College in 1932, leading to its accreditation by the American

Miner Teachers College on Georgia Avenue, Washington, DC—now part of the School of Education at Howard University. *Courtesy of University Archives, University of the District of Columbia*

Students at Miner Teachers College in the 1950s. *Courtesy of University Archives, University of the District of Columbia*

Association of Teachers Colleges. The library was named the Myrtilla Miner Memorial Library, and the building in which it sits still serves today as part of the School of Education at How-ard University.

Following court-ordered desegregation in the 1950s, which required that black and white students be educated together in the same institutions, the school merged with the all-white Wilson Teachers College to become the District of Columbia Teachers College. Through another round of mergers in 1975, the school was absorbed by the University of the District of Columbia, a fully accredited undergraduate, graduate, and pro-fessional institution of higher learning. At UDC Myrtilla's vision

Desegregation

The abolition of slavery and the granting of citizenship to African Americans (through the Fourteenth Amendment of the Constitution in 1868) were only the first steps in a long road toward racial equality in the United States. In many ways that equality still has not been achieved. Beginning in the late 19th century, the stated law regarding race relations in America was "separate but equal." In other words while African Americans were falsely proclaimed to be equal under the law, they were barred from white society in nearly every way. Black citizens were denied the same basic fundamental rights and privileges as white people. Separate bathrooms and water fountains for "colored" people were found all across America, and blacks were segregated from whites in housing, transportation, employment, and education. Nowhere was segregation more prevalent than in schoolrooms. African American students were denied access to white schools and colleges and were forced to attend underperforming institutions that did not offer the same opportunities as those offered to white students. In the early 1950s, however, attitudes began to slowly change and civil rights for African Americans finally were being discussed. In 1954 the US Supreme Court held, in the landmark case of *Brown v. Board of Education*, that separate schools for black and white students was unconstitutional. Though the difficult struggle for racial equality continues to this day, desegregation of American society had finally begun.

continues to this very day, and in her memory Miner Elementary School on 15th Street NE in Washington, DC, still inspires young students to learn the lessons of merit and equality.

———◆———

Ellen O'Connor did her best to contact Myrtilla's living friends and relatives in preparation for her book. She gathered as many letters and documents as she could find relating to the School for Colored Girls, and sometime around 1880 she began writing. Her own work with the school and her personal relationship with Myrtilla herself gave Ellen many unique and interesting insights that would form the basis of her biography, titled simply *Myrtilla Miner: A Memoir*. "This little volume," as Ellen affectionately called the final book, was published in 1885 by Houghton Mifflin and stands today as a warm tribute to the life and work of a courageous educator.

About 32 years after warning Myrtilla of the perils of opening a school for African Americans in Washington, DC, Frederick Douglass admitted to Ellen his shame in not being more helpful to Myrtilla when she first came to him for advice. "I never pass by the Miner Normal School for Colored Girls in this city," he wrote, "without a feeling of self-reproach that I could have said aught to quench the zeal, shake the faith, and quail the courage of the noble woman by whom it was founded, and whose name it bears." Years later, at the dedication of a Washington, DC, high school, Frederick once again related his first meeting with Myrtilla and reflected upon her legacy. "Some of her pupils still reside here and are among our most respected members of society. . . . I for one feel bound to hold her in grateful memory."

As Ellen finalized her memoir, she was saddened that Myrtilla's final resting place had still not been marked with a headstone.

It seemed improper that Myrtilla, flawed perhaps as she was, had not been appropriately honored in death. Through Ellen's efforts and the help of others who admired Myrtilla's work, a dignified monument to her memory was finally erected at the gravesite, identifying forever this noble woman. In an address to the students of Miner Teachers College in 1949—the 20th anniversary of its founding—one speaker rightly observed that a grave monument, no matter how appropriate, could not measure the legacy of a person or the radiance of a life. "*You* are that monument," said the speaker as he looked out over the gathering of African American students, "you who believe in and live for the human family in one world—you who with patience live high above the problem to become its answers."

At the time Ellen published *Myrtilla Miner: A Memoir*, there were in fact 98 graduates of the Miner Normal School—64 of whom were then employed as teachers in the public school system of Washington, DC. In the coming years, it is estimated that Myrtilla's school, in its various forms, graduated no less than 40,000 scholars, and through the University of the District of Columbia—and dedicated teachers across the country—her legacy continues to this day.

ACKNOWLEDGMENTS

———•◆•———

The writing of Myrtilla's story was, as with most books, a collaborative effort resulting from many sources. History comes alive only with penetrating research, the conduct of which no author could complete alone.

I would first like to thank Christopher Anglim, associate professor, archivist, and reference librarian at the University of the District of Columbia, for his gracious and patient assistance amid a torrent of inquiries. He provided or directed me to a variety of primary and secondary sources about Myrtilla Miner, he cross-referenced facts and statistics, and he supplied several of the images used in the book. I am indebted to Chris for all his help.

Joellen ElBashir, curator and interim chief librarian at Howard University, was very helpful in retrieving the speeches of Frederick Douglass as they related to Myrtilla Miner, and I am grateful for her assistance. My thanks also to the University of Rochester Department of Rare Books, Special Collections, and Preservation for researching and providing the fascinating correspondence between Myrtilla and William Seward. For assistance and insight into Myrtilla's relationship with Harriet Beecher Stowe I wish to thank Ellen Shea, head of research services at the Schlesinger Library, Radcliffe Institute for Advanced Study at Harvard University, and Elizabeth Burgess, collections manager at the Harriet Beecher Stowe Center.

Dawn Schontag, reference librarian at the Morse Institute Library in Natick, Massachusetts, was very helpful in coordinating the interlibrary loan of the Myrtilla Miner Papers from the Library of Congress, as was Jeffrey Greenburg for his microfilm review, collation, and copy of those materials for use in the book, and I thank them both. I also thank my friend Jimmy Ross, for his technical advice and assistance.

I thank Denise Roe, clerk of Madison County; Judy Engle, president of Limestone Ridge Historical Society; Dick Williams of the Clinton Historical Society; and Dot Willsey of the National Abolition Hall of Fame and Museum for their research and supply of local documents pertaining to Myrtilla's early life.

For her thorough reading of the initial manuscript I thank my good friend Juliette Chait.

Lastly, I thank Myrtilla Miner for being my writing muse for this book. Through pain, illness, rejection, threats of harm, and poverty she persisted in her quest to open her school, and her work serves as an inspiration to us all.

RESOURCES FOR FURTHER EXPLORATION

Miner Building at Howard University
Built in 1913 and located at 2565 Georgia Avenue NW in Washington, DC, Miner Building was the original site of Miner Teachers College. The building is currently used by Howard University's School of Education. A plaque to the right of the front door reads:

MYRTILLA MINER
BORN 1815   DIED 1864
ESTABLISHED EDUCATION
FOR
COLORED GIRLS IN THE
DISTRICT OF COLUMBIA

University of the District of Columbia
www.udc.edu/about/history-mission
Myrtilla's school merged into UDC in 1975 and carries on her legacy today. The university website contains an interesting

history of the school from the founding of Myrtilla's school through the present day.

National Abolition Hall of Fame

www.nationalabolitionhalloffameandmuseum.org

Located at 5255 Pleasant Valley Road, Peterboro, New York, the National Abolition Hall of Fame and Museum's stated mission is to "[honor] antislavery abolitionists, their work to end slavery, and the legacy of that struggle, and to complete the second and ongoing abolition—the moral conviction to end racism." Myrtilla Miner was a 2013 inductee to the National Abolition Hall of Fame.

The Harriet Beecher Stowe Center

www.harrietbeecherstowecenter.org

The Harriet Beecher Stowe Center preserves Stowe's Hartford, Connecticut, home, informs the public of Stowe's life and accomplishments, and "inspires commitment to social justice and positive change."

The Emancipation Proclamation at the United States Archives

www.archives.gov/exhibits/featured-documents
/emancipation-proclamation

The original Emancipation Proclamation signed by Abraham Lincoln on January 1, 1863, is housed in the National Archives in Washington, DC.

Seward House Museum

www.sewardhouse.org

Located at 33 South Street, Auburn, New York, the Seward House Museum preserves the original home and artifacts of Myrtilla's friend William Seward.

Frederick Douglass National Historic Site
www.nps.gov/frdo/index.htm
The Washington, DC, home of Frederick Douglass is now a museum, located at 1411 W Street SE, dedicated to his life and work.

National Museum of African American History & Culture
https://nmaahc.si.edu
A Smithsonian museum, the NMAAHC, located at 1400 Constitution Avenue NW in Washington, DC, is exclusively dedicated to the documentation and preservation of African American life, history, and culture.

United States Department of Education
www.ed.gov
Established in 1980 the Department of Education's stated mission is to "promote student achievement and preparation for global competitiveness by fostering educational excellence and ensuring equal access."

Prudence Crandall Museum
www.cultureandtourism.org/cct/cwp/view.asp?a=2127&q=302260
Located at 1 South Canterbury Road, Canterbury, Connecticut, the Prudence Crandall Museum is the former home and school of "Connecticut's State Heroine."

National Organization for Women
https://now.org
NOW is a social and political organization dedicated to women's rights and issues, located at 1100 H Street NW, Suite 300, Washington, DC.

National Civil War Museum

www.nationalcivilwarmuseum.org

Associated with the Smithsonian Institution and located at One Lincoln Circle, Harrisburg, Pennsylvania, the National Civil War Museum serves as a national center "to inspire lifelong learning of the American Civil War" through the preservation and presentation of wartime artifacts and scholarship.

NOTES

Prologue: To Preserve a Memory

"Myrtilla Miner [was] one of": Henry Wilson, *History of the Rise and Fall of the Slave Power in America* (Boston: Houghton Osgood, 1879), 2:583.

"I loved her very much": Ellen M. O'Connor to Isaac Miner, 28 March 1886, Myrtilla Miner Papers, Manuscript Division, Library of Congress, Washington, DC (hereafter referred to as "Miner Papers").

"a superb woman": Sherry Ceniza, *Walt Whitman and 19th-Century Women Reformers* (Tuscaloosa: University of Alabama Press, 1998), 207, quoting "Equal Suffrage Notes," *Sunday Providence Journal*, July 23, 1911.

"equal suffragist" and *"one at birth"*: Ceniza, *Walt Whitman*, 207, quoting "Equal Suffrage Notes."

"The love & affection": Nel O'Connor to Myrtle Miner, 5 September 1861, Miner Papers.

"You have often urged me": Ellen M. O'Connor, *Myrtilla Miner: A Memoir* (Boston: Houghton Mifflin, 1885), 20–21.

Chapter 1: A Country Girl

"little more than": O'Connor, *Myrtilla Miner*, 9.

the Nineteenth Township: Michael P. Martin, "Myrtilla Miner," *Madison County Heritage* 27 (2002): 17.

Seth helped found: Denise Roe, "'A Natural Right to Knowledge,'" *New York* Archives 12, no. 4 (Spring 2013): 24.

"the family was subjected": O'Connor, *Myrtilla Miner*, 10.

"curiously poetic": Myrtilla Miner, "written c. 1825," untitled and undated essay, Miner Papers.

"on account of": Miner, "written c. 1825." Historian Lester G. Wells pointed out that the darkness of the town's hemlock forests may also have been the reason for the tasteless nickname (Lester G. Wells, "To Teach the Darkened Child: Life and Letters of Myrtilla Miner," unpublished manuscript, undated, Miner Papers, 6).

"a man of uncommon": O'Connor, *Myrtilla Miner*, 10.

"You wonder": Miner, "written c. 1825."

"There is nothing": Myrtilla Miner, undated essay on "natural scenery," Miner Papers.

"Here I could see": Miner, "written c. 1825."

"A plan of female education": Thomas Jefferson to Nathaniel Burwell, 14 March 1818, in *The Writings of Thomas Jefferson*, vol. 15, (Washington, DC: Thomas Jefferson Memorial Association, 1905), 165.

she even sewed together: Lester G. Wells, notes of interview with Robert Goff and Marian Goff Pond, 6 September 1941, Miner Papers.

"the principles of": Myrtilla Miner to "My dear father," 10 December 1845, Miner Papers.

"This could only": Miner, "written c. 1825."

These institutions began: Leonard I. Sweet, "The Female Seminary Movement and Woman's Mission in Antebellum America," *Church History* 54, no. 1 (March 1985): 43.

"It was indeed": O'Connor, *Myrtilla Miner*, 12.

"I doubt not": Myrtilla Miner to "my dear Father, Mother & sister Achsa," 8 November 1839, Miner Papers.

"geography of the heavens": Miner to family, 8 November 1839.

"Health pretty good": Miner to family, 8 November 1839.

"rich and pleasing": Miner, "natural scenery."

"They were received": Wells, "To Teach," 20, quoting *Catalogue of the Young Ladies Domestic Seminary, Clinton, N.Y., 1833–1841, with the Valedictory Address of the Principal, March 31, 1841* (Whitesboro: Press of the Oneida Institute, 1841), 4.

"I was quite sick": Myrtle Miner to "Cherished-precious ones," 27 January 1840, Miner Papers.

"the heroic kind": O'Connor, *Myrtilla Miner*, 13.

"I think . . . the remedy": Miner to "Cherished-precious ones," 27 January 1840.

Chapter 2: Awakening

"Will you, sir": Myrtilla Miner to Gov. Seward, 18 December 1841, University of Rochester Rare Books & Special Collections (hereafter referred to as "Rochester Collection").

"40 young Ladies": Myrtilla Miner to Gov. Seward, 24 December 1842, Rochester Collection.

"the overpowering responsibility": Miner to Seward, 24 December 1842.

"Perhaps you will recollect": Miner to Seward, 24 December 1842.

"maturity of thought": William H. Seward to Miss Miner, 28 December 28 1842, Rochester Collection.

"My sympathies are always": Myrtilla Miner, undated essay on "Adaption," Miner Papers.

"Now don't begin to talk": E. G. Miner to "Oh My Sister," 31 March 1844, Miner Papers.

"Just come on and I will": Mary Atwater to "My Gentle Coz," 17 March 1844, Miner Papers.

"He told me the last time": S. Atwater to "Cousin Myrtilla," 27 November 1844, Miner Papers.

"scholar of the educational awakening": Sadie Daniel, "Myrtilla Miner: Pioneer in Teacher Education for Negro Women," *Journal of Negro History* 34, no. 1 (January 1949): 32.

"one of the best systems": Bernard C. Steiner, *Life of Henry Barnard: The First United States Commissioner of Education, 1867–1870* (Washington: Government Printing Office, 1919), 56.

"I tell you positively": Seth Miner to "Dear daughter Achsa," 14 February 1845, Miner Papers.

"My attention was called": Myrtilla Miner to "Dear Friends," undated (subject: "heart history"), Miner Papers.

Chapter 3: Mississippi

A loyal follower of Horace Mann: Wells, "To Teach," 56, quoting American Council of Learned Societies, *Dictionary of American Biography*, vol. 6 (New York: C. Scribner's Sons, 1933).

"South West" through *"I have a sort of NOTION"*: Wm. B. Fowle to Miss Myrtilla Miner, 23 June 1846, Miner Papers.

"that abominable war": Maria to Myrtilla, 13 February 1847, Miner Papers.

"slightly controversial": S. T. Martyn to Miss. M.M., 25 January 1847, Miner Papers.

"every thing to think of": Molly to "My dear Mrytle," 22 February 1847, Miner Papers.

"A slave is one who": John Bailey, *The Lost German Slave Girl: The Extraordinary True Story of Sally Miller and Her Fight for Freedom in Old New Orleans* (New York: Grove, 2003), 61, quoting Article 35 of the Civil Code (Wheelock S. Upton and Needler R. Jennings, *The Civil Code of the State of Louisiana with Annotations* [New Orleans: E. Johns, 1838]).

"A vigorous and comely mulatto girl": William H. Herndon and Jesse W. Weik, *Herndon's Life of Abraham Lincoln* (Cleveland: World Publishing, 1930), 63–64.

"beyond all reach of": Fowle to Miner, 23 June 1846.

"a finishing school for": Philip S. Foner and Josephine F. Pacheco, *Three Who Dared: Prudence Crandall, Margaret Douglass, Myrtilla Miner—Champions of Antebellum Black Education* (Westport, CT: Greenwood, 1984), 107.

"is not surpassed by any" and *"the Trustees of the Institute"*: William Kimbrough Pendleton, *The Millennial Harbinger*, vol. 6 (Bethany, Virginia: Printed by A. Campbell, 1842), 47–48.

"It is desirable that every pupil": Rules of Newton Female Institute, undated document, Miner Papers.

"The sound of the lash": O'Connor, *Myrtilla Miner*, 16.

"unjust, unnatural, and barbarous": G.W.(N?)C. to Myrtle, 30 May 1847, Miner Papers.

"In heaven's name my dear Myrtle": G.W.(N?)C. to Myrtle, 30 May 1847.

"mental sufferings": Myrtilla Miner to Gerrit Smith, Esq., 16 December 1847, Miner Papers.

"They are but grown up children": Miner to "Dear Friends," "heart history."

"calm, penetrating discussions": Miner to "Dear Friends," "heart history."

"Wherever I go": M. Miner to Doctor Phares, 26 July 1847, Miner Papers.

"If properly managed": "A New Plan of Negro Emancipation,"
Miner Papers. The author of the plan was Dr. Phares, but it
appears to be written in Myrtilla's hand. The document was
enclosed in MM's letter to Gerrit Smith of 16 December 1847.

"properly instructed": Miner to "Dear Friends," "heart history."

many enslaved people had been whipped: See, for example, Alison
Stewart, *First Class: The Legacy of Dunbar, America's First Black
Public High School* (Chicago: Lawrence Hill Books, 2013), 13.

"them first" and *"In that hour"*: Miner to "Dear Friends," "heart
history."

Chapter 4: "The Antislavery Altar of My Country"

"The truth is": M. Miner to Dr. Phares, unknown date, Miner
Papers.

"immediate unconditional emancipation": Gerrit Smith to Miss
Myrtilla Miner, 10 January 1848, Miner Papers.

"I address you, Sir" and *"may be accomplished surely and nobly"*:
M. Miner to William Seward, 1 January 1848, Rochester
Collection.

"like a great grief": Miner to "Dear Friends," "heart history."

"a miserable skeleton": M. Miner to Hon. Wm H. Seward, 25
December 1850, Rochester Collection.

"At last, the combined moral": O'Connor, *Myrtilla Miner*, 17.

"to the elevation and welfare": O'Connor, *Myrtilla Miner*, 18.

"The condition of women and slaves": La Vonne Marlene Siegel,
"Myrtilla Miner: Educator and Founder of the Colored Girls
School in Washington, D.C." (unpublished master's thesis,
George Washington University, June 1970), 20, quoting Pau-
lina W. Davis, untitled article in *Una*, April 1855, 57.

"The celebration of Independence": Myrtilla Miner, "The Celebration of Independence" essay, 4 July 1850, Miner Papers.

"*The safety of the country*": Miner to Seward, 1 January 1848.

"*to undertake so vast a work*": M. Miner to Hon. Gerrit Smith, 11 February 1850, Miner Papers.

"*I could give no satisfactory reply*": Miner to Smith, 11 February 1850.

"*dart off in another tangent*": Maria to "My dearly loved Myrtle," 10 May 1849, Miner Papers.

"*What shall we hear of you next*": Maria to Myrtilla, 13 February 1847.

"*There was a spirit of intense interest*": Wells, "To Teach," 113.

"*I think you misjudge me*": Achsa to "My dear sister," August 1849, Miner Papers.

"*Perhaps you think I love you best*": "Sister Achsa" to "Dear Sister Myrtle," 21 July 1849, Miner Papers.

"*If you are not going to teach there*": Achsa to "My dear sister Myrtle," 10 December 1849, Miner Papers.

"*I am quite willing to go*": Achsa to Myrtle, 10 December 1849.

"*Now, sir*": Miner to Smith, 11 February 1850.

"*No measure for the security of slavery*": O'Connor, *Myrtilla Miner*, 29.

"*I am now sitting in the sick room*": Charles Atwater to Myrtle, 21 July 1850, Miner Papers.

"*choking grief . . . and intense pain*": Myrtle to "Dear Friends, George and Louisa," 28 September 1850, Miner Papers.

"*I half think I will return to Providence*": Myrtle to George and Louisa, 28 September 1850.

"*As the time passed on*": O'Connor, *Myrtilla Miner*, 115–116.

"*slavocracy*": M. Miner to Gerrit Smith, Esq., 17 February 1850, Miner Papers.

"*Gangs of slaves, handcuffed together*": O'Connor, *Myrtilla Miner*, 31.

"*sufferers in this guilty city*": "An Account provided to Harriet Beecher Stowe in 1852 Giving a History of the Founding of the School," Miner Papers.

"*If an influence can be felt*": Miner to Seward, 25 December 1850.

"*friend to humanity*": Miner to Seward, 25 December 1850.

"*afflicted . . . & down-trodden*": Miner to Seward, 25 December 1850.

"*Although* in *Washington*": William H. Seward to Myrtilla Miner, 7 January 1851, Rochester Collection (emphasis added).

"*that in it was no word*": M. Miner to Hon. Wm. H. Seward, 21 January 1851, Rochester Collection.

"*I propose nothing new in principle*": Foner and Pacheco, *Three Who Dared*, 117, quoting Myrtilla Miner to E.D.E.N. Southworth, 16 May 1851, Miner Papers.

"*Our intention is to educate a class*": Myrtilla Miner to Peter Robertson Family, 31 July 1851, Hubbard-Robertson Family Papers, William Clements Library.

Chapter 5: "I Shall Try It!"

"*unyielding will when sure*": "Account provided to Harriet Beecher Stowe," Miner Papers.

"*I thought a school could be*": Miner to "Dear Friends," "heart history."

"*moral courage*": O'Connor, *Myrtilla Miner*, 25, quoting Miner to Mrs. Ford, 15 February 1851.

"*think your benevolent scheme*": Emma D.E.N. Southworth to Myrtilla Miner, 23 August 1851, Miner Papers; see also, Foner and Pacheco, *Three Who Dared*, 117.

"*I have to be very particular*": John F. Cook to Myrtilla Miner, 31 July 1851, Miner Papers; Foner and Pacheco, *Three Who Dared*, 116; Siegel, "Myrtilla Miner," 30.

"presumptuous in the highest degree": Miner to "Dear Friends," "heart history."

"for the protection of the Abolitionists": Miner to Smith, 17 February 1850.

"It was my custom to continue my work": All quoted material from Douglass found at O'Connor, *Myrtilla Miner*, 22–24.

"I shall try it!": Frederick Douglass, speech at the dedication of the M. Street High School, 1891, Archibald H. Grimke Papers, Moorland-Spingarn Research Center, Howard University.

"So you are the little woman": Cindy Weinstein, ed., *The Cambridge Companion to Harriet Beecher Stowe* (New York: Cambridge University Press, 2004), 1.

"saved us all from": Miner to "Dear Friends," "heart history."

"The thought is a great one": Miner to "Dear Friends," "heart history."

"The very remembrance of it today": Miner to "Dear Friends," "heart history."

"no one replied encouragingly": Miner to "Dear Friends," "heart history."

"Impelled by a sense of duty": Miner to "Dear Friends," "heart history."

Chapter 6: "National Only in Name"

"Washington, as compared with many": Frederick Douglass, *A Lecture on Our National Capital* (Washington: Smithsonian Institution Press, 1978), 21.

"Every negro and mulatto": Worthington G. Snethen, *The Black Code of the District of Columbia in Force September 1st 1848* (New York: William Harned, 1848), 38; Kate Masur, "Washington's Black Codes," *New York Times*, December 7, 2011.

"capable, very good": Emmett D. Preston, Jr., "The Development of Negro Education in the District of Columbia, 1800–1860," *Journal of Negro Education* 12, no. 2 (Spring 1943): 192.

"by far the ablest educator": *Report of the Board of Education to the Commissioners of the District of Columbia* (Washington: Government Printing Office, 1906), 108.

"Every person in the city": Louis P. Masur, *1831: Year of Eclipse* (New York: Hill and Wang, 2001), 3.

"The black men passed": Thomas Wentworth Higginson, "Nat Turner's Insurrection," *Atlantic*, August 1861, 176.

"the white people had commenced": Higginson, "Nat Turner," 179.

"A party of horsemen started": Higginson, "Nat Turner," 179.

When Snow himself couldn't be found: Jefferson Morley, "The Snow Riot," *Washington Post*, February 6, 2005.

In 1831 she established: Foner and Pacheco, *Three Who Dared*, 7.

"By this act": Foner and Pacheco, *Three Who Dared*, 9.

"High School for young colored": Foner and Pacheco, *Three Who Dared*, 12.

Chapter 7: "The School for Colored Girls"

"Character is what the age calls for": O'Connor, *Myrtilla Miner*, 113.

"Be as wise as serpents": "Weekly Critiques," written by Emily Howland, 22 November 1858, E. Bruce Kirkham Papers, Ball State University Archives and Special Collections, Alexander M. Bracken Library (hereafter referred to as "Kirkham Papers").

"an entire stranger in the community": Myrtilla Miner, *The School for Colored Girls, Washington, D.C.* (Philadelphia: Merrihew and Thompson's Steam Power Press, 1854), promotional brochure, 6, Miner Papers.

"the majesty of righteousness": Miner, *School*, 6.

"*official reasons*": J. N. Cary to "Ladies," 4 December 1951, Miner Papers.

"*Allow me to suggest*": Michael Flusche, "Antislavery and Spiritualism: Myrtilla Miner and Her School," *New York Historical Society Quarterly 59*, no. 2 (April 1975): 157, quoting A Democrat to Mr. Fillmore, June or July 1852, Miner Papers.

"*How beautiful my school*": Siegel, "Myrtilla Miner," 32.

"*The present promise is*": Miner, *School*, 6–7.

Perhaps most concerning to her: Daniel, "Myrtilla Miner," 36.

"*I do unequivocally assert*": Miner, *School*, 6.

"*to a point beyond that which*": L. F. Dewey to "My dear young friends," 2 May 1853, Miner Papers.

"*She gains the heart of some*": S. A. Shorter to "My Teacher," 12 May 1853, Miner Papers.

"*I will be learned*": Lizzie Snowden to "Dear Teacher," 6 April 1853, Miner Papers.

"*Though men enslave the body*": Mary Brent to "My Teacher," 14 May 1853, Miner Papers.

"*I hope Mrs. Dewey will not*": Emily M. Fisher to "My Teacher," 11 May 1853, Miner Papers.

She exposed her "scholars": Siegel, "Myrtilla Miner," 34.

On several occasions: Siegel, "Myrtilla Miner," 34.

One Northern publisher: Foner and Pacheco, *Three Who Dared*, 121.

During one such trip: Siegel, "Myrtilla Miner," 34.

"*The two little Girls*": M. A. Jones, "The two little Girls," 19 April 1854, Miner Papers.

"*I rise early and toil late*": O'Connor, *Myrtilla Miner*, 38.

"*I should be delighted*": M. Miner to Hon. Wm. H. Seward, 15 December 1851, Rochester Collection.

Soon other wealthy Philadelphians: Foner and Pacheco, *Three Who Dared*, 125.

"All must have failed": "Account provided to Harriet Beecher Stowe," Miner Papers.

"The malignant and jealous spirit": O'Connor, *Myrtilla Miner*, 32.

"nearly out of town": Foner and Pacheco, *Three Who Dared*, 122.

"because I would teach": O'Connor, *Myrtilla Miner*, 39.

"Thou will not of course": Samuel Rhoads to Ms. Miner, 15 March 1852, Miner Papers.

"turn out that nigger school": All quoted dialogue in this exchange is taken from "Account provided to Harriet Beecher Stowe," Miner Papers.

"When opposition and persecution came": Miner to "Dear Friends," "heart history."

"If it is [God's] work": O'Connor, *Myrtilla Miner*, 39.

"Miss Miner you will remember": Siegel, "Myrtilla Miner," 36.

"I think our Teacher is very kind": "Your Dutiful Scholar Mary Thomas" to "Dear Teacher," 1 February 1853, Miner Papers.

"I love my teacher very much": Siegel, "Myrtilla Miner," 77, quoting Lizzy Snowden to "Kind Friends," 10 March 1852, Miner Papers.

"On you more than on any other": "Weekly Critiques," 22 November 1858, Kirkham Papers.

Chapter 8: Growing Pains

"I love this school": O'Connor, *Myrtilla Miner*, 41.

In the first four months of 1853 and *"It is really an attractive"*: Foner and Pacheco, *Three Who Dared*, 146.

"The educational movement of those": Foner and Pacheco, *Three Who Dared*, 126.

Through these efforts: Foner and Pacheco, *Three Who Dared*, 128.

"a small frame house and barn": O'Connor, *Myrtilla Miner*, 46.

"noisy, boisterous, stormy, and fatiguing": O'Connor, *Myrtilla Miner*, 43 (emphasis added).

"*indiscretions and eccentricities*": Miner to "Dear Friends," "heart history."

"*Her perfectionism and self-righteousness*": Flusche, "Antislavery and Spiritualism," 162.

"*She was often severe in her kindness*": O'Connor, *Myrtilla Miner*, 110, 112.

"*became a standing joke*": Foner and Pacheco, *Three Who Dared*, 133.

"*In spite of all your faults*": Foner and Pacheco, *Three Who Dared*, 136, quoting Myrtle Miner to Walpole Cecil, 5 September 1853, Miner Papers.

"*How I wish I could take*": Foner and Pacheco, *Three Who Dared*, 136, quoting Myrtle to "My dear Maggie," 2 April 1853, Miner Papers.

"*When the school did open*": O'Connor, *Myrtilla Miner*, 47.

"*Why, I never see nicer looking scholars*": O'Connor, *Myrtilla Miner*, 48.

"*with a heart filled*": Myrtilla Miner to "Dear Miss Stowe," 1 October 1853, Miner Papers.

"*She has been gifted by nature*": Harriet Beecher Stowe to the Ladies Anti-Slavery Society of Glasgow, 18 November 1853, the Harriet Beecher Stowe Center, Hartford, Connecticut.

"*in a most forlorn and desolate condition*": O'Connor, *Myrtilla Miner*, 51.

"*If you are not out of that house*": "Account provided to Harriet Beecher Stowe," Miner Papers.

"*Emily and I lived here alone*": O'Connor, *Myrtilla Miner*, 51.

"*hard-to-get-over*": O'Connor, *Myrtilla Miner*, 51.

"*Mob my school!*": O'Connor, *Myrtilla Miner*, 56.

"*She was one of the bravest women*": O'Connor, *Myrtilla Miner*, 56.

Chapter 9: Exhilaration and Exhaustion

"Sometimes I think that slavery": Marietta T. Hill to "Dear Teacher," 5 July 1854, Miner Papers.

"Her school became": O'Connor, *Myrtilla Miner*, 84.

"We are now prepared to speak": Miner, *School*, 3.

"She has manifested": Miner, *School*, 9.

"suitable building": Normal School for Colored Girls, pamphlet, December 1856, Miner Papers.

"How scrupulously neat": O'Connor, *Myrtilla Miner*, 110.

"Here is something being done": Frederick Douglass, "Miss Miner and Her School for Colored Children in Washington," *Frederick Douglass' Paper*, September 1, 1854.

"so nearly white as to make": Douglass, "Miss Miner."

"My strength & faith almost fail": Siegel, "Myrtilla Miner," 62, quoting Myrtilla Miner to "All," 14 January 1855, Miner Papers.

"If you continue to conflict": M. Miner to "Dear Parents," May 1855, Miner Papers.

"partial derangement of the brain": Foner and Pacheco, *Three Who Dared*, 171, quoting Miner to M. Burleigh, 17 October 1856, Emily Howland Additional Papers, Cornell University Library, Ithaca, New York.

"I was a pitiable invalid": O'Connor, *Myrtilla Miner*, 85–86.

"Her hands, without any will": Gail Hamilton, *Gail Hamilton's Life in Letters*, ed. H. Augusta Dodge (Boston: Lee and Shepard, 1901), 1:234.

"Utterly worn and exhausted": O'Connor, *Myrtilla Miner*, 118.

"She gave the impression": O'Connor, *Myrtilla Miner*, 118–119.

"At present under God": Harriet Beecher Stowe to Myrtilla Miner, 8 November 1855, Miner Papers.

Chapter 10: "William the Unlucky"

"invalid teacher": Emily Fisher to Myrtilla Miner, 26 November 1855, Miner Papers.

"I am quite well again": O'Connor, *Myrtilla Miner*, 86.

"A True Woman": Mary J. Capron, "Miss Lydia B. Mann 'A True Woman,—Strong, Pure, Patient,'" *Education: A Monthly Magazine Devoted to the Science, Art, Philosophy and Literature of Education* 10 (September 1889–June 1890): 472.

"William the Unlucky": Foner and Pacheco, *Three Who Dared*, 158.

"There are in the United States": *Normal School for Colored Girls*, December 1856.

"to erect a larger and more suitable": G. Smith Wormley, "Myrtilla Miner," *Journal of Negro History* 5, no. 4 (October 1920): 450, quoting "School For Free Colored Girls in Washington," *Boston Journal*, April 18, 1857 (emphasis added).

"an unjust and dangerous interference": All quoted material from the Lenox letter found in O'Connor, *Myrtilla Miner*, 63–71, quoting Walter Lenox, "To the Editors," *National Intelligencer*, May 6, 1857.

Lenox was, at the time: O'Connor, *Myrtilla Miner*, 73.

"the high tide which pro-slavery feeling": O'Connor, *Myrtilla Miner*, 58.

"Ex-Mayor Lenox's letter appeared": Druscilla J. Null, "Myrtilla Miner's 'School for Colored Girls': A Mirror on Antebellum Washington," *Records of the Columbia Historical Society, Washington, D.C.* 52 (1989): 267, quoting William H. Beecher to Samuel Rhoads, 14 September 1857, Miner Papers.

"a real old fogy": Foner and Pacheco, *Three Who Dared*, 164, quoting statement from Myrtilla Miner written on correspondence from L. D. Gale, Miner Papers.

Chapter 11: "A Perpetual and Impassable Barrier"

"that unfortunate race" through *"a perpetual and impassable"*: Dred Scott v. Sandford, 60 U.S. 393 (1857), 407.

"Miss Howland is a host in herself": Myrtle to "My dear friend," 7 November 1857, Miner Papers.

"I have walked myself so lame": O'Connor, *Myrtilla Miner*, 89.

"I am anxious you should": O'Connor, *Myrtilla Miner*, 90.

"I have made frequent inquiries": Lester Grosvenor Wells, "Myrtilla Miner," *New York History* 24, no. 3 (July 1943): 370, quoting Millard Fillmore to Myrtilla Miner, 31 March 1858, Miner Papers.

"could kindle a fire": "Weekly critiques," 22 November 1858, Kirkham Papers.

"any further correspondence": Samuel Rhoads to Myrtilla Miner, 14 July 1859, Miner Papers.

"It is pleasant to see": Myrtle to "My dear friend," 7 November 1857.

"If I teach others": Foner and Pacheco, *Three Who Dared*, 188, quoting Emma Brown to Myrtilla Miner, 8 February 1858, Miner Papers.

Chapter 12: This Noble Woman

"excellencies and defects": "Weekly critiques," 1 November 1858, Kirkham Papers.

"popped catlike upon us": Foner and Pacheco, *Three Who Dared*, 191, quoting Emily Howland to "Dear folks at home," 2 February 1859, Emily Howland Papers, Division of Rare and Manuscript Collections Cornell University Library (hereafter referred to as "Howland Papers").

"I have told M. Miner": Foner and Pacheco, *Three Who Dared*, 191, quoting Howland to "Dear folks at home," 2 February 1859, Howland Papers.

"I do not like or respect": Dorothy Sterling, *We Are Your Sisters: Black Women in the Nineteenth Century* (New York: W. W. Norton, 1997), 201, quoting Emma V. Brown to Emily Howland, 29 November 1860, Howland Papers.

"We understand that the colored people": Foner and Pacheco, *Three Who Dared*, 193, quoting Bowen to Howland, 17 September 1859, Howland Papers.

"awful fury": Lester Grosvenor Wells, "Myrtilla Miner," *New York History* 24, no. 3 (July 1943): 370, quoting Myrtilla Miner to Dear Friends, 13 May 1860, Miner Papers.

"The shadows of the approaching": O'Connor, *Myrtilla Miner*, 99.

"There is a noble woman": Wilson, *Rise and Fall*, 2:582.

"grand conflict": Myrtle to "My blessed brother N. & Wife," 9 December 1862, Miner Papers.

"immediately assumed the appearance": Myrtle to "Dear brother," 27 April 1861, Miner Papers.

"[I] stood near Mr. Lincoln": Myrtle to "My dear brother," 13 March 1861, Miner Papers.

Over 1.5 million Americans: Flusche, "Antislavery and Spiritualism," 170.

"This person does not look back": Myrtle to "My dear friend," 7 November 1857.

"If the spirits can so far control": Foner and Pacheco, *Three Who Dared*, 191, quoting Bowen to Howland, 17 September 1859.

"Citizens Friends": Emily Howland, notes, undated, Miner Papers.

"animal magnetism" through *"save their children"*: Clippings from unidentified California newspapers, Miner Papers.

"The angels guide me": Myrtle to brother and wife, 9 December 1862.

"Having done what I could": Myrtle to brother and wife, 9 December 1862.

"You three have the confidence": Foner and Pacheco, *Three Who Dared*, 198, quoting Bowen to Howland, 31 May 1862, Howland Papers.

"Her majesty": Foner and Pacheco, *Three Who Dared*, 198, quoting Bowen to Howland, 31 May 1862, Howland Papers.

"I never, in my life": Doris Kearns Goodwin, *Team of Rivals: The Political Genius of Abraham Lincoln* (New York: Simon & Schuster, 2005), 499.

"I trust that from this time forth": Foner and Pacheco, *Three Who Dared*, 198, quoting US Congress, Senate, Senate Resolution 536, *The Congressional Globe: Containing the Debates and Proceedings of the Third Session of the Thirty-Seventh Congress* (Washington, DC: Congressional Globe Office, 1863), 1326.

"to educate and improve": An Act to Incorporate the Institution for the Education of Colored Youth in the District of Columbia, Chap. CIII, 37th Cong. (1863).

"One thing is certain": O'Connor, *Myrtilla Miner*, 123–124.

"The Almighty certainly never intended": Martin Van Buren to President Andrew Jackson, 31 January 1829.

"I entered it with much exhilaration": O'Connor, *Myrtilla Miner*, 125.

"profuse hemorrhage": O'Connor, *Myrtilla Miner*, 125.

"I was full of courage": O'Connor, *Myrtilla Miner*, 126.

"a dying woman": "The Miner School," unsigned and undated newspaper article, Miner Papers.

"There is something touchingly impressive": Wilson, *Rise and Fall*, 2:586.

"Within this lowly grave": *Report of the Board of Education*, 129.

Epilogue: "You Are That Monument"

"If Myrtilla Miner's spirit": Octavius Brooks Frothingham, *Memoir of William Henry Channing* (Boston: Houghton Mifflin, 1886), 405.

"an institution which offered": Miner Teachers College Catalogue (Washington, DC: Public Schools of the District of Columbia, 1947–1950), 16, Miner Papers.

"This little volume": O'Connor, *Myrtilla Miner*, v.

"I never pass by": O'Connor, *Myrtilla Miner*, 24–25.

"Some of her pupils still reside here": Douglass, speech at M. Street High School.

"You are that monument": Paul F. Douglass, "Changing the Minds of Men," March 9, 1949, Founders Day Address, Miner Teachers College, Howard University (emphasis added).

BIBLIOGRAPHY

Books

Bailey, John. *The Lost German Slave Girl: The Extraordinary True Story of Sally Miller and Her Fight for Freedom in Old New Orleans.* New York: Grove, 2003.

Ceniza, Sherry. *Walt Whitman and 19th-Century Women Reformers.* Tuscaloosa: University of Alabama Press, 1998.

Foner, Philip S., and Josephine F. Pacheco. *Three Who Dared: Prudence Crandall, Margaret Douglass, Myrtilla Miner—Champions of Antebellum Black Education.* Westport, CT: Greenwood, 1984.

Frothingham, Octavius Brooks. *Memoir of William Henry Channing.* Boston: Houghton Mifflin, 1886.

Hamilton, Gail. *Gail Hamilton's Life in Letters.* Edited by H. Augusta Dodge. Boston: Lee and Shepard, 1901.

Herndon, William H., and Jesse E. Weik. *Herndon's Life of Abraham Lincoln.* Cleveland: World Publishing, 1930.

Jefferson, Thomas. *The Writings of Thomas Jefferson*. Vol. 15. Washington, DC: Thomas Jefferson Memorial Association, 1905.

Masur, Louis P. *1831: Year of Eclipse*. New York: Hill and Wang, 2001.

O'Connor, Ellen M. *Myrtilla Miner: A Memoir*. Boston: Houghton Mifflin, 1885.

Snethen, Worthington G. *The Black Code of the District of Columbia, in Force September 1st, 1848*. New York: William Harned, 1848.

Steiner, Bernard C. *Life of Henry Barnard: The First United States Commissioner of Education, 1867–1870*. Washington: Government Printing Office, 1919.

Sterling, Dorothy. *We Are Your Sisters: Black Women in the Nineteenth Century*. New York: W. W. Norton, 1997.

Stewart, Alison. *First Class: The Legacy of Dunbar, America's First Black Public High School*. Chicago: Lawrence Hill Books, 2013.

Wilson, Henry. *History of the Rise and Fall of the Slave Power in America*. Cambridge, MA: Riverside, 1879.

Magazines, Articles, Journals, Pamphlets

Catalogue of the Young Ladies Domestic Seminary, Clinton, N.Y., 1833–1841, with the Valedictory Address of the Principal, March 31, 1841. Whitesboro: Press of the Oneida Institute, 1841.

Daniel, Sadie. "Myrtilla Miner: Pioneer in Teacher Education for Negro Women." *Journal of Negro History* 34, no. 1 (January 1949): 30–45.

Douglass, Frederick. *A Lecture on Our National Capital*. Washington: Smithsonian Institution Press, 1978.

Douglass, Frederick. "Miss Miner and Her School for Colored Children in Washington." *Frederick Douglass' Paper*, September 1, 1854.

Douglass, Paul F. "Changing the Minds of Men." March 9, 1949. Founders Day Address, Miner Teachers College, Howard University.

Flusche, Michael. "Antislavery and Spiritualism: Myrtilla Miner and Her School." *New York Historical Society Quarterly* 59, no. 2 (April 1975): 149–172.

Higginson, Thomas Wentworth. "Nat Turner's Insurrection." *Atlantic*, August 1861.

Lenox, Walter. "To the Editors." *National Intelligencer*, May 6, 1857.

Martin, Michael P. "Myrtilla Miner." *Madison County Heritage* 27 (2002): 17–21.

Masur, Kate. "Washington's Black Codes." *New York Times*, December 7, 2011.

Morley, Jefferson. "The Snow Riot." *Washington Post*, February 6, 2005.

Null, Druscilla J. "Myrtilla Miner's 'School for Colored Girls': A Mirror on Antebellum Washington." *Records of the Columbia Historical Society, Washington, D.C.* 52 (1989): 254–268.

Preston, Emmet D., Jr. "The Development of Negro Education in the District of Columbia, 1800–1860." *Journal of Negro Education* 12, no. 2 (Spring 1943): 189–198.

Roe, Denise. "'A Natural Right to Knowledge.'" *New York Archives* 12, no. 4 (Spring 2013): 23–25.

Siegel, La Vonne Marlene. "Myrtilla Miner: Educator and Founder of the Colored Girls School in Washington, D.C." Unpublished master's thesis, George Washington University, June 1970.

Sweet, Leonard I. "The Female Seminary Movement and Woman's Mission in Antebellum America." *Church History* 54, no. 1 (March 1985): 41–55.

Wells, Lester Grosvenor. "Myrtilla Miner." *New York History* 24, no. 3 (July 1943): 358–375.

Wormley, G. Smith. "Myrtilla Miner." *Journal of Negro History* 5, no. 4 (October 1920): 448–457.

Archives, Collections, Documents, and Historical Papers

Grimke, Archibald H. Papers. Moorland-Spingarn Research Center, Howard University.

Howland, Emily. Additional papers. Cornell University Library, Ithaca, New York.

Hubbard-Robertson Family Papers. William Clements Library, University of Michigan, Ann Arbor.

Kirkham, E. Bruce. Papers. Ball State University Archives and Special Collections, Alexander M. Bracken Library.

Miner, Myrtilla. Papers. Manuscript Division, Library of Congress, Washington, DC.

Report of the Board of Education to the Commissioners of the District of Columbia. Washington: Government Printing Office, 1906.

Seward, William Henry. Papers. University of Rochester Rare Books & Special Collections.

INDEX

—◆—